# Beaten Odds

**Footprints of uncertainty, resilience, adventure and triumph**

Stephen Mabea
with
Joshua Araka

Copyright © 2020 Stephen Mabea and Joshua Araka

All rights reserved.

This publication may not be reproduced, in whole or in part, by any means including photocopying or any information storage or retrieval system, without the specific and prior written permission of the publisher.

This book is sold subject to the condition that it shall not, by way of trade or otherwise, be re-sold, hired out, or otherwise circulated without the author's or publisher's prior consent in any form of binding or cover other than that in which it is published and without a similar condition including this condition being imposed on the subsequent purchaser.

First Edition: October, 2020

Published by Nsemia Inc. Publishers (www.nsemia.com)

Cover Concept: Joshua Araka

Cover Photo Credit: Joshua Araka

Cover Design: Linda Kiboma

Layout Design: Bethsheba Nyabuto

Project Consultant: Matunda Nyanchama

Note for Librarians:

A cataloguing record for this book is available from Library and Archives Canada.

ISBN: 978-1-989928-05-9

"Either write something worth reading or do something worth writing."

~ **Benjamin Franklin**

# DEDICATION

This book is dedicated to my family, my pupils and the people of Kenya

# Table of Contents

Dedication .................................................................................. v
Foreword ................................................................................... ix
Prologue .................................................................................... xi

**1. THE FOUNDATIONS ........................................................... 1**
   The Light ............................................................................. 3
   Ababembe Clan .................................................................. 13
   Resonance ........................................................................... 15
   Walk to destiny ................................................................... 25
   From Boy to Man ............................................................... 35
   Scaling the Heights ............................................................. 37
   The Love of My Life ........................................................... 47

**2. MY CAREER IN TEACHING ............................................. 57**
   My First Posting .................................................................. 59
   Aborted Trip ........................................................................ 77
   A Move to Nyansiongo ....................................................... 87
   Revitalizing Nyansiongo ..................................................... 95
   A selfless teaching staff ..................................................... 101
   Selfless pupils .................................................................... 105
   Destination: Kisii Primary School ..................................... 113
   Dealing with Segregation ................................................. 119
   Simeon Nyachae Takes Note ............................................. 123

**3. ADMINISTRATION IN EDUCATION ............................. 131**
   Another turn ...................................................................... 133
   Sweeping Irianyi ................................................................ 135
   My Inspection Duties ........................................................ 139
   Staffing Duties ................................................................... 141
   Ten Percent Recruitment .................................................. 145

**4. WHEN TROUBLE COMES ............................................... 151**
   Etale is kicked out ............................................................. 153
   My Encounter with Peter Oloo Aringo, MP .................... 159

## 5. MAZIWA YA NYAYO .......................................................... **167**
   The School Milk Programme ........................................ 169
   What Did I Go Home With? ......................................... 177

## 6. COMMUNITY SERVICE ................................................... **185**
   Politics, Trade and General Administration ................. 187
   Establishment of schools................................................ 193
   When Corruption Fought Back ..................................... 205
   Mecheo Location is Created ......................................... 211
   Church Matters ............................................................. 231
   Peace Keeping .............................................................. 239
   Nyamecheo Water Project & Water Matters................. 245
   Lighting the Villages..................................................... 251
   Tarmac Road.................................................................. 255
   Pilgrimage to Israel....................................................... 263

## 7. CONCLUSION.................................................................... **269**
   Where was my Family?.................................................. 271
   Our School System........................................................ 275
   If I Were to Reverse the Clock!..................................... 277

# FOREWORD

*Beaten Odds* draws deep, exciting and thought-provoking experiences in the life of Mzee Stephen Mabea. It brings forth the story of a Kenyan born into humble beginnings to newly converted Christians in pre-independent Kenya. It is a rich account of his adventures amid uncertainty in the Gusii countryside; his education in an environment that ascribed little value to schooling; a fulfilling career in the education sector, both as a teacher and administrator; community service in building schools and churches; a love for the Supreme Being; and respect and high regard for human life.

Like for any human being, Mabea's life had not been devoid of challenges. However, whenever he is confronted with such challenges, Mabea stays forward-looking, unbowed. In most instances, he gets the last laugh. It is a streak seen across his entire journey, be it in undertaking teacher training at Kabianga, leading successful schools of Nyansiongo (in newly created Borabu settlement scheme) and Kisii Primary School (in cosmopolitan Kisii Town), helping pyrethrum, coffee and tea farmers get a fair return for their sweat (in Motagara and Nyansiongo) or ensuring proper teaching standards through proper support for teachers in Kisii and Siaya. This is in addition to continuous community involvement.

The book captures rich, charming qualities ascribed to Mabea's life and his ability to spot opportunities and seize them for himself and those around him, while creating more pathways of advancement for others. It is an insightful life story of a humble man driven by honesty, dedication to service, high level professionalism, hard work, trust and immeasurable confidence to swim through and triumph in the face of challenges of life.

It leaves, to the reader, an impression of authenticity and candidness that drove Mabea to great heights of success in his work as a teacher, education administrator, community person and family man.

## Foreword

Mabea is a good example of what leadership entails, be it in the 'small' or 'big' roles we play in society. Raising a God-fearing family, moulding character in young ones rooted in proper ethics, empowering the masses and doing the little we can to make life better is the beauty of this life. Within this book, Mabea's account is proof that, regardless of our beginnings, one can achieve one's dreams when one puts God first and focuses on the goal of success.

In penning *Beaten Odds*, Mzee Mabea throws a challenge to us all: that of telling our stories! So told, these stories form the collective heritage to bequeath future generations from which they would draw, however little, lessons that could inform and enrich their lives.

*Beaten Odds* is a fast read. It has been written in a simple yet captivating style that makes it riveting. It is a book from whence the young, the old and future generations will forever draw lessons for their own lives. It is a simple guide to transformative and impactful and selfless leadership.

The story affirms that hard work, honesty, integrity and fortitude do not go unrewarded. Above all, there is overwhelming satisfaction when one does the right thing, at the right time and in the right manner.

SENATOR OKONG'O OMOGENI
SENATOR, NYAMIRA COUNTY

# PROLOGUE

One day I was walking with my wife along a path that links the family house to the farm. It was early Sunday evening and the clouds to the West clumsily hang under the sun. This provided us with the ideal weather for the walk. The rest of the sky was deep blue. Birds of the air went overdrive chirping from the many indigenous trees in the homestead. Midway, we unconsciously stopped to watch the birds as they jumped from one tree to the other while we tried to identify them by their names. Afterwards, we proceeded with our leisurely walk.

My wife is younger than me. However, due to bad health, she makes feeble steps than I do. I have therefore made it a routine to walk with her by my side as an exercise, morning and evening. This is what her doctor has recommended. The path is about 200 metres and as we walked, we reflected on the life we have lived since we became husband and wife.

As we looked back on the journey we had travelled so far, we found ourselves making a U-turn, back to the house. Elizabeth reminded me of our humble beginning as we stopped to admire the hills in the yonder, including Matunwa, Ikorongo and Nyansiongo. We could also see parts of Bomet County in the horizon. As all this happened, I recalled that we married when I had obtained college education, meaning that she never saw my real beginning.

Next to the family house is parking for a car, a poultry cage and a fish pond. My wife sat on the bench outside the house in our homestead. I made slow steps down the wooden staircase to the fish pond, their food in the hand. I stocked the pond a year earlier. As I approached, the fish popped up, expecting to get their feed. Indeed, this was their feeding hour.

I watched as the movement of the fish caused ripples in the water. The gently swaying water competed with the exuberant yells from a hen that had just laid an egg in a cage that sits adjacent to the pond. I realized that I was smiling. The hen had just laid an egg and it was informing every other creature in the compound! Perhaps to the hen, this was an achievement. I wondered what the hen would have done if it owned the 20 acre piece of land, the movable and immovable assets therein and all the family members associated with my humble roots.

Afterwards, I walked along the edge of the pond, letting the air blow as it wished. My job of feeding the fish done, I headed back to the house. As I took my favourite sitting position, my mind told me that I should tell my story. I had travelled an eventful journey from humble beginnings whose story I felt could interest others, and mostly my family and those in our community. I figured out that my story would be chronicled better when I am still alive. God has been good to me and given me a chance to put my life in its context, for myself, my family, the community and for posterity.

I was fortunate to get formal education. My father never had the same privilege that he accorded me. Perhaps, if he had it, he would have written a story about his life, about his family lineage and community. This way, we, his offspring, would be able to trace our history and add more chapters into it. Had my father written a book, it would have become a key reference material, at least to those of his progeny. But how would he have done that, yet he neither knew how to read nor write, let alone how to go about it?

I shared my thoughts with my family that evening. My children, led by Zablon were very receptive and told me that I should have finished telling the story, in written form. He was ready to go to any distance, to have this dream achieved, with God's providence. This got me challenged even more. The journey of writing this book had just started!

This journey has been exciting and challenging too. Piecing the information from the time my parents wedded, all through to the stages of life that I have gone through has been a wonderful experience. It reminded me of the highs and lows, the hits and misses, the friends I made, the challenges I encountered along the way and how I overcame them.

I discovered that keeping records is a noble idea. Indeed, the documents in my archives played a critical role in solidifying and verifying several aspects of the story. The photos that I took at various occasions added value into this mission.

Due to my advancing age, there are a number of names of persons I interacted with that eluded my mind. The same applied to exact dates that particular events occurred. This called for patience in reaching out to those people directly or using contacts close to them. Many of them were very supportive and gave me information that enhanced this story. And there are many others we wished to reach out to but who, unfortunately, had preceded us to the yonder, called by our Maker.

I have to salute my family, the pupils I interacted with during my teaching days, the teachers I worked with, the parents of the children I taught and nurtured, and everyone whose life I touched directly or indirectly during my sojourn in education, the community and church. These are the people who gave me the experience, exposure and a story to tell. Without them, my story would be empty! I particularly thank those who gave information that validated various segments of what I tell in this book.

Having said that, let me add that any errors one may find herein were not intended. I take full responsibility for their commission or omission.

I do not understand how this story would have panned out had I told it singlehandedly. As a matter of fact, it would have been a more herculean and daunting task for me. This is why my family reached out to Joshua Araka to assist me in giving this assignment a professional touch. Araka exhibited a high level of patience, order and clarity in ensuring we walked together through my life and delivered this story in a form that can enable understanding and, hopefully, be captivating for the reader.

I equally thank Dr. Matunda Nyanchama of Nsemia Inc. Publishers who came to my home and assured me that my dream was attainable. I credit him for giving me a glimpse of

*Prologue*

what this story would be like at that initial stage. Indeed, his word reinforced my vision and I am happy that we now have my story in form of a book.

Thank you for getting hold of this book. I hope you will enjoy reading it! I hope it would enrich your life, even if only in a small way.

Barikiwa Sana!

*Stephen Mabea*
*Mecheo, Borabu*
*August, 2020*

# 1. THE FOUNDATIONS

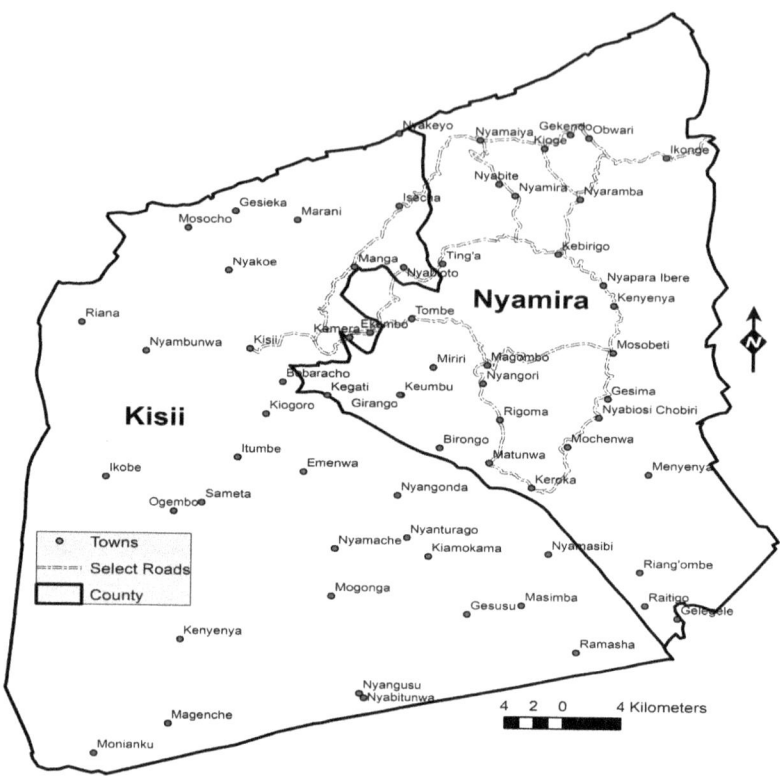

Kisii & Nyamira Counties: Map Credit: Kefa Otiso

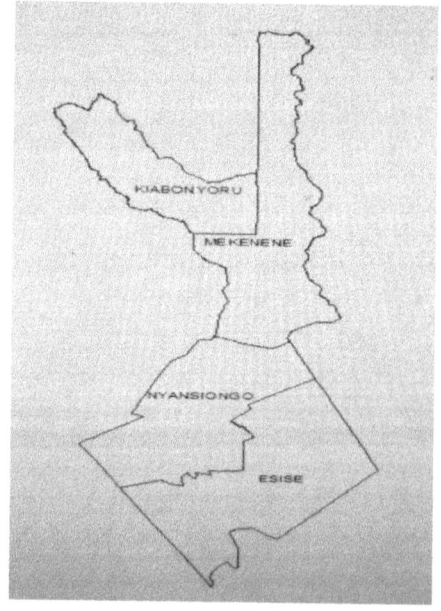

Borabu Constituency: Map Credit: Kefa Otiso

# The Light

When the brides and the grooms walked down the aisle, matching to the tunes of the accordion, excitement filled the church. Save for the aisle and the pulpit, the Lord's house was jam-packed. There were as many people seated on the benches as those who stood behind them. Many others peeped through the windows and the rear door to catch a glimpse of the historic event. Among the brides and the grooms ready to take their marriage vows that momentous day in 1933 were Gatimel Gisore Mabea (Arieri) and the love of his life Atalia Nyachoke. At the time, nobody knew that the two were going to be my parents two years later.

In that ceremony, there were many brides and the grooms, and as many as twenty couples. These young men and women were members of Seventh Day Adventist (SDA) Church that had been introduced by the British Missionaries in Kisii.

On that day of my parents' wedding, they were accompanied by their friends, relatives and curious members of the community from various corners of the then South Kavirondo District. The district covered the present day Kisii, Nyamira, Migori and Homa Bay counties. South Kavirondo was initially split into Homa Bay and Kisii Districts. This model of provincial administration was scrapped when Kenyans passed a new constitution in 2010, paving way for the creation of counties.

In the colonial times, the former Nyanza Province was called Kavirondo. Its boundaries were wider than they are known today. For instance, parts of present day Kericho County were under Nyanza Province. These were later moved to Rift Valley Province. A section of residents have felt over time that the boundaries were controversially reviewed. Those who hold this view do so in the understanding that in the past, their forefathers used natural features and landmarks such as hills, valleys and rivers as boundaries. This was tampered with by surveyors who introduced beacons. As a result, over time, people from various ethnic communities near or along the former natural boundaries have held contrasting viewpoints on the surveyors' job. This has affected places such as Chemilil at the Kericho-Kisumu border. Another example is the Bomet-Borabu border. However, I will not dwell on this matter for it was not the driving force for penning this book.

My parents wedded at a church that is close to the Nyanchwa SDA Conference. This is the pioneer conference of the church in Gusii. Today, there is a church in most places in the two counties of Kisii and Nyamira. At the time, however, the faithful travelled miles and miles, on foot, to reach their places of worship. The area had a poor road network and vehicles were a rare sighting. This meant that whenever there was a major church function at Nyanchwa, majority of the members from within the borders of the conference rose up early in the morning to be there on time.

My late father hailed from Bobembe within the Abagichora sub-clan in the present-day West Mugirango constituency of Nyamira County. Bobembe is about thirty kilometres to Motagara in Bosamaro sub-clan where my late mother was born. This means that my father and mother's homes were not less than fifty kilometres to the wedding venue, Nyanchwa.

But how did they meet? My father was a regular church goer at Nyanchwa. For my mother, she was lucky to be introduced to formal education. She was a pupil at Nyanchwa Girls' School that was introduced in 1922[1]. Indeed, religion and education made it possible for them to meet at Nyanchwa, and ultimately culminated in their union in marriage just as it did for many couples.

I find it interesting that the distance from their homes to Nyanchwa and lack of vehicular means of transport did not deter the two to meet the expectations of their hearts. None of this was going to be an excuse for them not to wed in the church, as the denomination's guidelines provided.

---

1   See Prof. Mary Getui's *The establishment and history of the activities of the Seventh Day Adventist (SDA) Church among the Abagusii of Western Kenya 1918 – 1985;* Masters' Thesis; School of Religious Studies, University of Nairobi, 1985.

There were mixed reactions when the congregants spotted my father. Unlike the other grooms, my father was sharply dressed in a sparkling white shirt, short trousers and black shoes. To some, my father's haircut and clearly shaven beard completed the picture of a handsome young man. But others thought otherwise. Some wondered in hushed tones and others openly; was this man going to keep his wife and raise a stable family if he could not afford long trousers for the wedding?

Those who held this view glanced at him from the head to toe and back. Some sneered while others laughed without a care. My father did not have cotton in his ears and he clearly heard the ridiculing remarks. However, he chose to ignore the voices, hold his head high, take the vows, tie the knot and take his wife home.

In Gusii of that time, it was perceived that people who hailed from Bogirango clan, like my parents, were poorer than residents of Nyaribari and Kitutu where majority of the brides and grooms at the wedding came from. So, the congregants literally judged and condemned my father for opting to wed in the church. Why? They had judged a book by its cover. To them, he was a poor man going by the level of his dressing. One could make the inference that, to the onlookers, weddings should have been a reserve of people of means, even within the local standards then.

They appeared to suggest that it could have been wiser if my late parents just made a 'come we stay marriage' arrangement or became enjoined through a traditional wedding ceremony which was cheaper and could be done closer to their homes. This, they seemed to suggest, should have been better than looking odd by walking down the aisle in the midst of grooms dressed in long trousers while my father was in a pair shorts.

Naturally, many people like judging others and making assumptions based on looks. The congregants neither knew my father's plans nor his financial muscle. They did not know that, unlike his peers who were dressed to kill but did not budget for a bouquet and a small reception after the wedding, my father was prepared for the same. He had prepared well for his big day but the plans were very close to his chest and close friends who were integral in the planning.

When the pastor declared the grooms and the brides as husbands and wives, there was ululation. Outside, the attendees appeared to have favour for the newly wedded couples except my parents. However, there was a change in their attitude when they discovered that my father had bought several crates of soda and loaves of bread for his guests.

Within human limits, it is easier to endear oneself to someone once you have taken care of his stomach. This is how people who had been gossiping my father in hushed voices changed the narrative. They now seemed to suggest that it was wiser for a groom to feed his guests than spend extravagantly on clothes and let them return home yawning and eager to lay their hands on a meal once there. My late parents and their entourage must have obviously reached home weary that evening, having covered the entire distance on foot.

*****

Prof. Mary Getui has this to say about the first SDA church that was established at Nyanchwa on the outskirts of Kisii Town:

> "...taking the message to Gusii was one R. Evanson, an English missionary. With the help of Jakobo Olwa, they set up the first mission at Nyanchwa in 1912. Olwa was a Luo teacher who had been converted to Adventism and was now sent as a missionary. In 1913, Carsallen opened another Adventist station at Kamagambo, at the Gusii-Luo border. Of the two, Nyanchwa was to have more influence on Abagusii."

Following the establishment of this first SDA church, the gospel, as propagated by the missionaries was fast getting ingrained in the hearts and nerves of the people of Gusii. This saw a quick rise in church membership which compelled the leadership to open more churches to take care of the newly converted.

The leadership had operationalized a strategy where converts converged and stayed at a particular place for prayer and worship while broadening the number of God's 'fishers of men'. Just as we are told today, the British missionaries told the people that their creator, God, resided in heaven. They also assured them that God would send his only son Jesus who had died for their sins back to the earth soon. Jesus would pick the faithful and go with them to heaven. Therefore, people needed to abandon sin and get ready for the advent of the son of God.

With the good stories flying around about the happy life in the yonder, the gospel gained momentum fast. Followers of the church stayed together in encampments *(chikambi)* that were composed of temporary huts (*ebigutu*) where they worshipped God for a period running to weeks or months; some of these would later become permanent settlements for those residing there. The first encampment was started at Nyaguta in Kiogoro. The place is about 7 km from Kisii Town along Kisii-Kilgoris road. The encampments attracted church members from the breadth and width of Gusii.

Ideally, these encampments were camp-outs. Adults would move in, together with their children to receive the word of God and strengthen their faith. I remember that my parents often carried me and covered the distance on foot to Nyaguta. This was despite the fact that our home and the encampment place were over 30 km apart.

The number of followers swelled quite quickly. There was also concern that, with no vehicular transport, some were covering mind-boggling distances to Nyaguta. This necessitated the opening of another encampment area at Ogango in Kitutu Masaba constituency. Situated a stone throw away from Nyaikuro junction along Kisii-Chemosit road, Ogango served members of the church from the upper part of Gusii (Nyamira) who included our family.

However, it is important to note that at this stage, I had grown substantially big. I was a pupil at Motagara Intermediate School and could join other youths at Ogango for spiritual matters. As time progressed, the church opened another camp area at Kebirigo. This was nearer home than Ogango and we were very happy. Other pioneer camp centres were opened at Sironga and Kenyenya, much later. With the opening of more camp centres, the idea of *ebigutu* collapsed. Church members gradually stopped staying in the encampments and would operate from their homes.

My parents were among those from our area in Bobembe who moved to the Kenyenya Church grounds in present-day Nyamira County when it was first established. The church encampment comprised of huts neatly lined with each family allocated a hut of their own.

While there, the converts mainly prayed, read and memorised Biblical verses every day. They also sang songs of praise and did some work in their farms. It appears to me that the preachers of the time had initially done a good job in convincing the converts to abandon the comfort of their homes and to stay in the fortified site to strengthen their faith and prepare for the second advent of their Maker.

Converts also learnt matters of nutrition and keeping high standards of hygiene. The latter were incorporated in the weekly routines in the encampments. It included time for prayer, observing the start and end of the Sabbath, and routine inspections to ensure that all homes were kept clean.

Child mortality was very high in pre-independent Kenya. Among other causes, children died due to debilitating pneumonia attacks shortly after birth. There were many still births as well. This was obviously a gut wrenching and disappointing experience especially to young couples. It could get worse. In some cases mothers died at childbirth. It is due to the relatively high child mortality that mothers bore a large number of children.

*****

I did not skip the story of my birth. One day in January 1935, I joyfully cried to announce my arrival in the world. I was birthed in the Kenyenya church compound in the presence and with the assistance of my mother's fellow women who midwifed the process.

My mother would later recount to me how the women's ululations drowned my cry as she held her bundle of joy. She told me that this joyous moment when I joined the family made her even more prayerful. She told God to protect me from evil and let me survive. To her, there were indications through gut feeling that I was going to survive. My survival would give her a wonderful experience of raising me up.

In the Bible, a story is told of a man called Stephen. The book of Acts 6:8 says, "And Stephen was full of faith and power, did great wonders and signs among the people."- *Holy Bible, Gideon's Version.* The book expounds however, that Stephen was deeply dedicated to the Lord. He was accused of blasphemy and was stoned to death. This happened after he was given a chance to renounce his faith and out-rightly declined.

Such a strong believe in the Lord is unmatched and has been quoted and preached over the years. Perhaps this is what informed my parents' decision to give me this special name from the Bible. They named me Stephen Mabea Arieri.

Equally, the name Mabea is significant to the family because it was my grandfather's name. As was the tradition, it was proper for me to get a family name on top of the Christian one. Having been duly named, I was then dedicated to the Lord in the church by elder Isaac Simi. Just as it happens today, my parents were instructed by the church elder to give me healthy food and never introduce me to alcoholic drinks and harmful drugs. Elder Simi also counselled my parents to bring me up within the confines of Christianity. I have stayed in the faith ever since. I believe that I never digressed much despite the many temptations of this world.

We did not stay long in the camp compound at Kenyenya. Pastor Webster, a Briton posted to minister in the camp, argued that the idea of members staying in the encampment was bound to harm them in the long run. Instead of the converts staying in one place, he proposed that they go out and acquire parcels of land for themselves just as the other members of the community were doing.

True as Webster reasoned, many people who were yet to convert to Christianity were busy taking up free land. For instance, due to migration, some members of Ababembe clan had occupied virgin land at Nyabisimba. This area was virtually a thick forest and grassland. Animals roamed there freely, the dominant ones being wild cats *(ebisimba)* that were notorious for feeding on chicken. Etymologically therefore, the name of Nyabisimba is derived from these cats. It loosely translates to, 'a place of wild cats'. These cats were very many especially along Nyabisimba stream that originates at the top of Nyabisimba hill and bisects the village.

Among the early settlers at Nyabisimba was my father's elder brother Aori. My uncle Aori had not seen the reason and purpose for embracing Christianity. In fact, he was secretly wooing my father to get out of the church encampment and acquire land as well.

So, at the time of Pastor Webster's counsel, my father had strategically excused himself from the camp and acquired himself a piece of land at Nyabisimba. This was made possible by his brother Aori who hived part of the land he had acquired and gave it to him (my father). The thick brotherly love that flew in Aori's veins also made him allocate my father a hut in his compound. As fate would have it, this hut provided us initial accommodation when we left the church encampment. Nyabisimba is a place with lush green vegetation on a gentle terrain. It is about five kilometres from where I was born. It is also not far from my mother's childhood home.

One of the major teachings of the SDA Church is that a man should be married to one wife. According to the Adventist' doctrine, polygamy is greatly detested. Presently, the church manual provides penalties for engaging in polygamy. According to the teachings, the church leadership has powers to strike off the name of a member from the church register for engaging in polygamy and other practices which contravene the SDA doctrines. Such a member is then given a chance to repent his sins and be re-baptised before he is re-admitted into church membership.

I am not sure if this was the case when my father 'backslid' in his faith and took in more wives. By the time he died in 1994, he was survived with four wives, including my mother, several children and grandchildren. My mother's co-wives are Sibia Kemuma, Rebecca Motondo and Nyanchama Nyaega.

My father's polygamous status did not distract his dream of raising a united and God-fearing generation. Although he later abandoned attending church services, my father was a very strict and enterprising patriarch who insisted that all his wives and children grow up guided by Christian values. These values, which include honesty and integrity, are ingrained in our extended family and run in the blood of the majority of us.

# MY FAMILY TREE

Below is my family tree tracing back to the Ababembe clan patriach

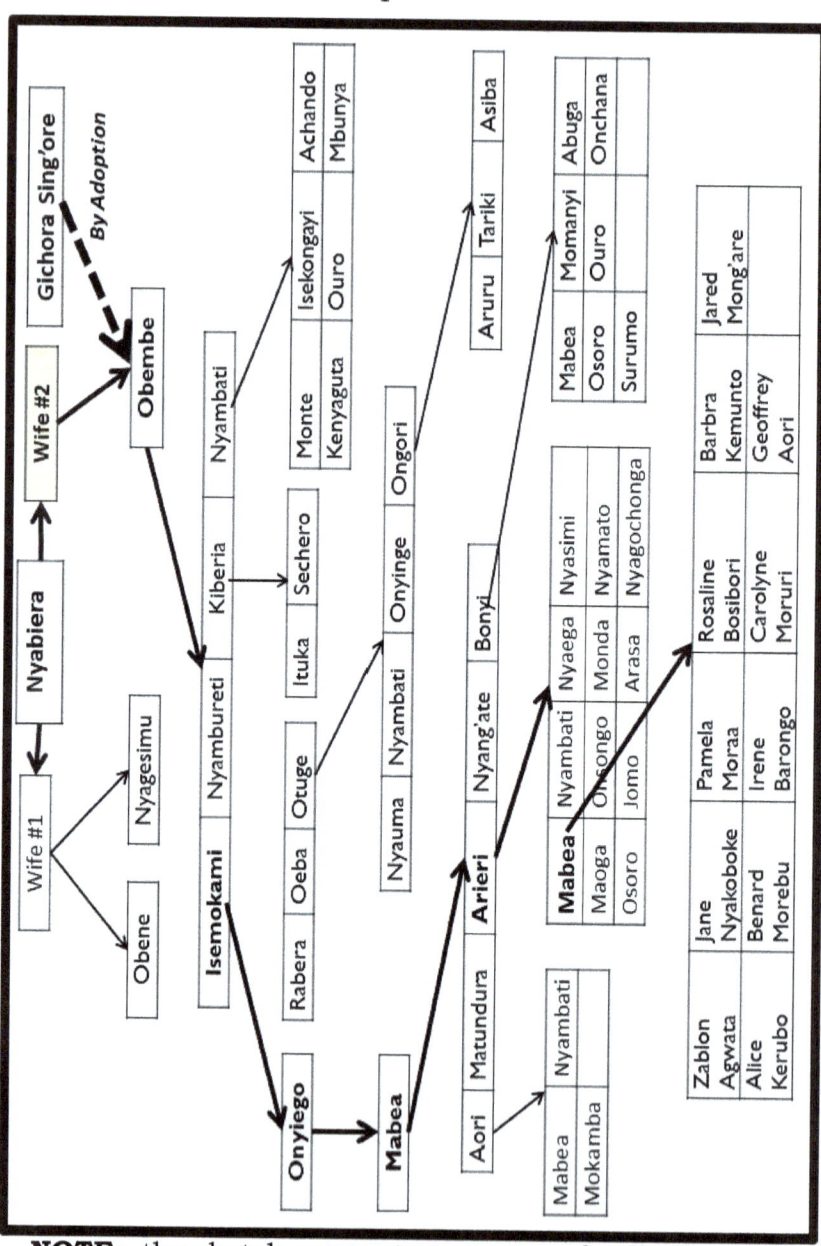

**NOTE:** the sketch concentrates on my family line with names captured in bold

# Ababembe Clan

I belong to Ababembe clan which is part of the larger Abagichora clan by assimilation. A member of the clan is referred to as *Omobembe* (singular) and *Ababembe* (plural). Like the wild seed, presently, Ababembe are spread across many parts of the world. And it is not by accident. The sub clan has a rich migratory story.

From oral tales, their history can be traced to farther than Bogetaorio in Marani Sub-County, Kisii County. As a matter of fact, available details of this history are scant. However, it has it that Nyabiera who had his roots in the Kipsigis (part of the larger Kalenjin) community had two wives. The first wife had two sons: Obene and Nyagesimu. The second wife had one son, Obembe.

At the time, Abagusii and the Kalenjin often fought, particularly over land and livestock. The Kalenjin who were more adept at war and had relatively sophisticated crude weaponry could strike Gusii villages and drive away cattle. The Gusii would retaliate and return their cattle on a lucky day. The confrontations were often bloody and tragic.

When Nyaberia and his wives died, Obembe was caught up in one the ethnic face-offs and was captured by Kalenjin warriors. They managed to go with him to a place in present-day Kericho County, where he was assimilated into the Kipsigis community. Once he came of age, he got married and had two wives. One day, for unknown reasons, Obembe assembled his family for a party. After the feasting, he bid them good bye and embarked on a journey back to his roots. The risky journey in the bushes through Ikorongo in Nyaribari Masaba took him several days, perhaps weeks. For unclear reasons again, and my guess is that it was due to the fact that he was an orphan, Obembe did not head straight to Bogetaorio. Instead, he ended up in Keera area of West Mugirango, Nyamira County.

Once at Keera, he was received and adopted by one Gichora (the father of Abagichora clan) who swiftly arranged for Obembe to get a wife. Soon, Obembe got married to Monyangi and started a new family within the homestead of Gichora. It means that at that stage, his father Nyaberia's family was scattered. Thus, Obembe had his step-brothers at Bogetaorio while his children and two wives remained in Kericho, and he was now in Keera. The descendants live in those places to date. However, due to assimilation, his family in Kericho has been swallowed in terms of language and all other aspects of life. The Obembe in West Mugirango equally got assimilated by Abagichora, the descendants of Gichora.

Currently, most of the descendants of Obembe live in Nyameru, Otanyore, Getiesi and Nyabite within Keera location. However, some moved and settled in other areas such as Geta, Nyabiosi, Nyaikuro and Nyabisimba. All these are within the borders of the expansive Bogichora clan in Nyamira County. Others have settled away from Bogichora. You will also find some of them in Nyansiongo, Mecheo and Mogusii areas of Borabu Constituency. Still others have settled in Kitale, Tranz-Nzoia County, among other areas of the country and the globe.

# Resonance

Jeffrey Fry, author of *Distilled Thoughts*, is a renowned philosopher in the United States of America. Fry must have thought great and hard when he said that, "to realize that all people are alike and all are different is the beginning of wisdom." Fry's wisdom resonates well with a story from my early days.

While we were toddlers, many people in our community realized that Elkanah Omanwa and I looked alike. We were born in the same month and our mothers were close friends. Whenever the two went to the market, they bought us identical clothes. Often times, we were dressed exactly the same way.

One evening, women in the community had a meeting. As usual, Omanwa's mother carried him along to the meeting. My mother too carried me and when they settled for their discussions, they left us to play. At the time, I am told, we were barely one year.

Nobody could tell how it exactly happened that neither of the mothers was able to pick their child when the meeting ended. At night, Omanwa declined to suckle my mother's breasts just as I refused to be breastfed from his mother's. Instead, each of us cried incessantly that night and denied the adults the peace of a good night's sleep.

Questions arose the following morning, amid fears that, perhaps, we had fallen sick. The mothers' hearts were filled with anxiety and they drew the attention of the men in the community to help them figure out what to do with us.

"This crying is not normal," Isaac Simi, the church elder who had earlier on dedicated me to God in church, reportedly said. "Would you swap the boys and see if they can stop crying?" he asked.

No sooner had the mothers obliged to Simi's suggestion than Omanwa and I stopped crying and reached for the breasts of our respective mothers to put to an end the hollowness that had been created in our stomachs for nearly fifteen hours.

For those witnessing it all, it was unbelievable! Apparently, we had confused our mothers who gave us strange breasts to suckle. The environment in the wrong houses too may have contributed to our respective unease.

This is a story that was told and retold during our days of growing up. Consequently, Omanwa and I were advised to love one another as twin brothers would. Indeed, we have kept the bond between us to this day. We grew up playing and consulting each other closely, knowing that if somebody hurt one of us, it equally affected the other.

I would be veering from the truth if I insist that we never went different paths at some stage. It was not our intention though. My friend Omanwa was unable to go for college education and opted to travel to Uganda where he worked as a lumberjack. I was lucky to join college and train as a teacher. I then got a teaching job and rose through the ranks to become an officer in charge of teacher school staffing in the former Kisii District. When I was a staffing officer, I thought this was an opportune time to have him back and help him secure a teaching job too.

Despite the fact that he had been away for many years, I was surprised that he was still as sharp as a razor on matters of teaching and he took the job with unequalled happiness and gratitude. He also showered me with unforgettable platitudes. Our paths had converged once again and I am happy because we both served the country in the education sector until we retired. As fate would have it, both of us were lucky to separately purchase pieces of land in the Borabu Settlement Scheme, located in Nyamira County, and bordering Bomet County. My friend Omanwa is now a senior citizen with a home in Kineni, not far from my home in Mecheo. We often visit each other to reminisce about our past and present experiences and wish ourselves well.

*****

When my father Arieri, his siblings Aori and Bonyi moved from Bobembe in Keera location to Embonga, there was nothing to tell that they would look at life differently. At the time, the drums of Christianity could be heard all over Gusii. Once at Embonga, my father moved to the SDA encampment at Kenyenya while his brothers settled down tending the land they had acquired. There were others like Aroni, Onyinge, Nyaigoti, Saruti and Asuga, who had all moved from Keera. They also contemplated joining the church but eventually did not do so. My father got baptised, a move that appeared to be a pre-condition to settle in the encampment at Kenyenya. While at Kenyenya, his brothers opted to permanently switch their homes from Embonga to Nyabisimba.

In some quarters, it is believed that members of the SDA church took the message that 'Jesus was coming soon' seriously. Those behind this school of thought believed that God would find them easily if they stayed at a common place. Many years down the line, and as a Christian and an Adventist, I still hold the belief that the second advent of the Lord is not far, for no-one knows the day or the hour of His return.

At the Kenyenya encampment grounds, my father joined hands with other youthful members like Isaac Simi who eventually became a pastor and Ishmael Ondieki who remained an ardent follower of the church. Equally, other young people like Osoro and Isaya took to Christianity as the fish takes to the water.

*****

Let me go back to what I mentioned earlier on and attempt to paint the scenario within which my parents met. From where I sit, I think that had it not been for Christianity, I doubt that my parents would have ever met and agreed to become husband and wife. Indeed, although they hailed from areas that were not that far from each other, I do not see anything else that would have made them to meet. However, as luck would have it, my mother Atalia was born to fairly forward-looking parents. They took her to a boarding school *(rirondo)* at Nyanchwa. At the time, education was a new idea in Kisii and the uptake was slow, especially for the girl child.

Nyanchwa Boarding Primary School had just started. Sponsored by the SDA church, the school accommodated learners from various places across Gusii. Most of them were children of new converts to the church. Nyanchwa was a central point on SDA-related religious issues. My father, then a youthful convert, would go there for religious gatherings.

On several of such visits, he spotted a beautiful, disciplined and dedicated young girl. The duo soon struck a relationship that culminated in a wedding. At the time, my mother would read and write as well as solve elementary questions. Her decision to drop out of school was not unwise given prevailing trends. As such, the move was not strange at the time. Indeed, many young men at the time married school going girls, who happened to be relatively mature, to transition into a new stage of life. If one dares do this in the modern-day Kenya, the wrath of the law would follow on him ruthlessly.

It should be clear that at the time, those who were reluctant to embrace Christianity stuck to tradition. They could offer sacrifices to appease the gods. This was an age-old practice. Whenever my father declined to join them in partaking the sacrifices, they thought he was running away from a good tradition that had been in existence for years. They also took more wives as was the norm, while my father stuck to one. But over time, he too slid from the teachings of the church and took in three more wives.

I noted earlier that my father was able to read the signs of the times and excuse himself out of the Kenyenya Church encampment to go and acquire a piece of land alongside his brothers. After placing the beacons, he returned to the camp. I think that he was finding it difficult to make a lasting decision. Instead, he chose to have one foot in the church and another outside. This indecisiveness was not strange, considering the situation he was in and the fact that he was among the few who were seen to be the light of the society at the time. He was in a dilemma. His peers were busy out there acquiring virgin land. They were also tilling the land and keeping their own cattle. Realistically, my father was going to remain behind in terms of wealth acquisition and advancement as per norms of the time. He also feared that, in such a sad eventuality, he would be perceived to be a young man who watched as poverty crept in to ensnare him for good.

Polygamy was also still deep rooted in the community. A number of my father's peers were into it, meaning that in the coming days, they would have bigger families. Indeed, at the time, the larger the family[1] one had, the more the respect that he was accorded. These issues troubled his mind.

My elder uncle Aori must have read the confusion his brother was sailing in. One evening, Uncle Aori sneaked into the camp while crickets chirped outside and ordered my mother to follow him with me on her back. Although I was barely three, I could see that my uncle was up to something. I could not tell if my mother was for this idea, but I did not see her make any attempt to oppose it. Perhaps, being a staunch Christian, my mother had reservations regarding the new path the family was venturing into. However, this was a time when wives' submissiveness to their husbands was deeply rooted in the community and invariably, the family followed the orders of the family patriarch – a father or the eldest son in the home. I suspect this is why she complied with the family patriarch's decision without any objection.

I was not afraid to travel in darkness because I was not alone. However, when we got to our new home, I was very scared. There was a goat in the room and I had never got close to one before. The sighting of the goat as it chewed the cud in the poorly-lit hut was the last thing I expected that evening. I vividly recall the appearance of the goat and how I reacted that night. I was apprehensive; scared to death and I clung to my mother all through the night! This has always made me tell my children who stay in towns to occasionally

---

1   **Editor's Note:** *large families meant one had many hands to work on the land and produce more. The man of the home (omogaka bw'omochie) also gained respect because of the fact that he was able to manage a large family; what with the inevitable ills such as competition, jealousy and others that are prevalent in such large families. It was also a bonus where there were many girls, for the family would reap big from dowry paid for the girls as they were married off.*

bring my grandchildren home so that they can familiarise themselves with domestic animals and life in the village in general.

I noted earlier that my father was torn between leaving the Kenyenya encampment and staying. However, his brother Aori's intervention made him decide to leave so that my father could also acquire land at Nyabisimba. My uncle was very supportive. Apart from giving my father part of the land he had acquired, he gave us a hut to start off our lives away from the encampment. Again, he gave us some poultry and food. This enabled us to adjust to the new life.

Looking back, my parents' decision to embrace Christianity at that very early stage was not in vain; it was good for the family on the whole. I say so because, when I look around, there is a very big difference between a family that embraced Christianity and that which did not.

For instance, in the past, the Gusii built round huts and never bothered giving the walls a smooth smear. Due to my father's stay at Kenyenya church encampment, he learnt from the missionaries a new way of constructing houses. Once he settled at Nyabisimba, he built a hut that had sharp corners. Above that, the hut was artistically thatched and the walls smeared using clay. This made it stand apart from other huts in the area, with people terming it *enyomba ya obosomi* (a Christian's house). As a result, people in the surrounding came in to have a glance of our hut and, over time, replicated the same in their homes. The day we moved to this particular hut is fresh in my mind to this day; it was most exciting, to say the least.

*****

The Kebirigo-Mosobeti-Metamaywa road, which has since been tarmacked, runs through our home in Nyabisimba and divides our land into two. The middle part of the land is fairly flat. This is the part that has been partly taken up by the road. I also donated a half an acre piece of land for Riamabea SDA Church. (A detailed story about the church and my other engagements in community service form part of fodder in Chapter Six of this book.)

The lower part of the land is steep on either sides and forms a depression in the middle through which a spring flows in majestic silence, emptying its water into the nearby river. On the upper side, the terrain is even steeper and, to my eyes then, it appeared to touch part of the sky. My family has donated part of the upper part for a secondary school whose story will come to you much later.

I have already noted that there was excitement at Nyabisimba when my father built his first house there. Every other house in the area and its environs was round and had a grass thatched roof. The earthen walls and floors of the houses were poorly made and were often times breeding grounds for jiggers and other parasites.

Although our house had similarities, it stood apart. Area residents regarded it an architectural masterpiece, what with its sharp corners and interior partitioning. The walls and floor were smoothly smeared and decorated using a special type of soil. As young as I was, I could see and overhear residents complementing my parents for building the house differently and being prayerful.

It is often said that 'imitation is the mother of invention'. Soon, our neighbours excitedly built houses similar to ours. Such houses have withstood the test of times to this day, albeit with varied and exciting modifications.

When I stood at the front side of our house, my innocent eyes stretched my sight to the hills in the distant horizon. Still, some hills like Nyamiranga appeared very close to our home. When I moved to the back side of the house, I realised that we were closer to the horizon and the sky appeared to rest at the edge of our land. All this made me imagine that the world was not any wider than I saw it.

One may suspect that the decision to withdraw ourselves from the Kenyenya Church encampment was an anti-climax, especially for my mother who had become staunchly Christian and active in the church. Well, it was not. She kept the spirit burning and ensured she excelled to be emulated by other women in the area.

When I look back, I feel that the vigour with which SDA members carry themselves has waned over time. In the days of yore, the Sabbath was strictly observed. The church had a bell ringer who sounded the bell at exactly 6 pm on Fridays. This signalled the start of rest and worship, which lasted an entire twenty four hours. He could then ring the bell once again at sunset the following day to mark the end of the Sabbath. In between, it was a near abomination for an Adventist to engage in any taxing and labour intensive activities at or away from home.

On Saturday mornings, Adventists congregated for fellowship. Then in the afternoon, you could hear them walking together while singing and beating drums. They spent the time visiting those who had not converted. They preached to this lot and prayed that they too could also join the church.

My parents' move to Nyabisimba had other influences and I have to credit them for taking the 'light' to the place. Many people in the area had never slept on mattresses spread on raised beds. They were happily astonished that time was ripe for them to gradually replace the cow skins which acted as their beds. They also started buying their sons pairs of shorts to cover their nakedness. At night, families started using kerosene lamps for lighting instead of wax wound on sticks, which they had been using.

*****

Renowned playwright William Shakespeare was on point when he said that the world is a stage and we mortals are mere actors. Indeed, when one's time to exit the world comes, he or she will surely go. But even in death, those of us alive nurse fond memories of our loved ones who have departed. I nostalgically remember my father who died in 1994 and my mother who followed him six years later. Both were at advanced stages of their lives, although I may not be able to be very specific in terms of their age.

Although my siblings and I are all mature, I have to admit that nobody can take the place of a parent. When a parent exits the world, there is a vacuum that can hardly be filled by any other human being. This is irrespective of the age of the parents.

My parents were not perfect but they were the best I could have had. They gave their all to mould me into a respectable, reliable and dependable person. They acted as springboards for my life and I owe them for all that I have.

In particular, my father was a jovial, forward looking and loving person. He valued education and wanted each of his children to acquire it. Although he backslid from the path of Christianity and could imbue traditional brews contrary to the teachings of the Church, he strongly encouraged us (his children) to be true to the church. He equally discouraged us from ever partaking in alcoholic drinks. He used to refer to our home as Jerusalem, the city in which Jesus was born. The name is still used by a number of people in the area.

I may not be the right person to qualify my fathers' rectitude. However, from my human eyes, my father was a good man. He worked hard in the farm, growing pyrethrum and tea. He got proceeds from the two to give my siblings and I an education, the best ever reward that a parent can give a child. Apart from that, he was a renowned herbalist, treating various health conditions including barrenness in women.

The image of my father dances in my head whenever I tell this story. I also hear his deep and authoritative voice ring in my ears. He was a tall black man and many people said that I was his replica. He walked energetically and cut a fatherly and patriarchal figure of the large family.

Some people say that sons have a softer spot for their mothers than their fathers. They also say that daughters think of their fathers before their mothers. To me, and for the purpose of this story, the comparison is neither here nor there. I loved my mother as much as I loved my father.

My mother was a tall, brown and harmless-looking beautiful woman. She was exceedingly religious and was the glue that bound the entire family together. When my father married other wives, my mother happily welcomed her co-wives and gave them a firm foundation characterised by hard work, resilience, the fear of God, and the love of education. This endeared her to them and their offspring.

Unlike my father, my mother had been introduced to formal education as alluded to earlier. She had a sharp memory and could read biblical verses and articulate issues with an allure of unmatched brilliance. Up to and during her sunset days, she recited memory verses with ease.

> **Biographer's note:** *Details of this chapter were validated in an interview with Mzee Mabea's brothers Philip Nyambati and Jephither Monda. Nyambati is Mabea's immediate follower while Monda is his step-brother.*

# Walk to Destiny

Of all pastime activities during my early days, I cherished playing hide and seek with my peers most of the time. We could also weave small fishing baskets then place them at particular spots along Nyabisimba stream in the evening to trap fish. At night, we retired to bed in the hope that the we would find several fish in the basket the following day. One had to be an early riser to go and check if the fish were foolish enough to enter the baskets. Being an early riser was the surest way of beating would be cunning boys who 'harvested where they had not sowed'.

Presently, Nyabisimba stream is a pale shadow of its former self. In my childhood, I enjoyed watching its waters dance rhythmically as it burbled and meandered on the steep agrarian terrain. When it reached flat ground, it appeared still and water beetles raced this way and that way, exciting my baby innocent eyes. The water volumes of the stream increased during the rains and submerged nearby vegetation. As the volumes increased, the ferocity too did. Then as the water hit the rocks and bends downstream, its ripples could be heard several metres away. As curious kids, we wished to get closer but our parents always cautioned us that the spring was angry and would swallow us. I wondered in silence if the water ever had a destination and if it ever got full.

I think if I spent more years fishing, I would have become a very experienced and skilled fisherman. Away from making baskets and using them to catch fish, I effectively used a fishing rod. This was a complimentary approach to the use of baskets. Our adventure as lads drove us to explore and know many other fishing methods.

For example, we knew particular fish breeding spots in the stream. When the water volumes reduced, we mobilised ourselves to make a concoction out of leaves of a particular indigenous shrub *(emechegechege)*. We then poured it in the spring, well aware that once the fish swallowed the water, they would float and make it easy for us to catch them. The downside of this mode of fishing was that it affected domestic animals whenever they drunk the water as they could diarrhoea, possibly to death. Often times, we roasted some of the fish and ate it before meal time because we knew that it was extremely delicious and our appetites would not wait. Additionally, fish was presumed to be a delicacy to be enjoyed mainly by children.

I remember this experience because I have lately ventured into fish farming in my farm in Mecheo. When I expressed my interest at the Borabu Fisheries extension office, the officers took me through fish farming training. They also helped me to sink a pond and stock it. The demand for fish is higher now than it was seven decades ago. Moreover, nutrition from fish is better appreciated now than when I was growing up; it is no longer children's delicacy but one for the entire family.

Today, Nyabisimba stream, just like many other springs and rivers in Nyamira County, are highly polluted. They have also reduced water volumes. Unlike in the past, the bed of the stream is visible to the naked eye. The pollution is due to the use of chemicals in farming. With erosion and leaching, these chemicals find their way into the river by rain water, destroying aquatic life in the process. In the past, I enjoyed watching water beetles playing in the spring. I also laugh when I recall that as children, we believed that girls' breasts grew big when bitten by the beetles. Sadly, I cannot recall the last time I saw a water beetle in the spring.

Apart from the use of chemicals in farming, several indigenous trees and bushes which grew along the springs and rivers have been cleared. These have been replaced by exotic water guzzlers like eucalyptus. Eucalyptus trees mature faster and are hard woods with several uses. These trees were introduced to the area when I was a little boy. They now make Nyamira look quite green but the truth is, the county has less water than it did when I was growing up. I agree that unless we put firm interventions in place, Nyamira will join the rest of humanity in the fourth world war which experts have warned that it will be over water. That said, I am happy that the county government is mobilizing residents to remove the trees from close to rivers, springs and wells, and replace them with water friendly plant varieties like bamboo.

*****

One day, I stopped to ponder as my mother carried water in an earthen pot from the spring. I had been playing when I saw her arrive with the pot delicately yet skilfully balanced on her head.

"*Omoisi' oyo* (you lad)! You need to go to school and learn many things, among them making pots," she said.

The next day, I embarked on a journey to kick illiteracy out of my head. Although I was barely four, I strongly believed that my mother was right; at school, I would learn several things.

Kenyenya Primary School was and still is a stone throw away from where I was born. Although it was about five kilometres from our Nyabisimba home, it was the nearest primary school anyway. The distance was not an issue for me because there were other children from our area with whom we attended school and returned home at lunch hour.

The country's education environment has evolved over time. In my early days, the curriculum started from Sub-Standard A[1]. One then proceeded to Sub-Standard B before joining Standards One, Two, and Three, in that order.

I vividly recall what Kenyenya Primary School looked like then. It had four classrooms and an office, all made of grass thatched roofs, earthen floors and walls. The grass used to make the roofs was particular and grew in wetlands and quagmires. The windows were mere ventilations and classrooms did not have lockable doors. I strongly doubt if a modern day child will sit in such a room to study. However, at that time, it was the best there was and we did not see any

---

1 **Editor's Note:** *Sub-Standard A and B can be equated to present-day Standard One and Two, respectively.*

problem with it. All we wanted was to satiate the burning desire within us for formal education.

I vividly recall my first teacher Mr. Joshua Simba. He was a tall, brown elderly man with a deep voice and a cheerful heart; he made me love school. And, as time progressed, his bravado made me love teaching. After all, teachers were the only professionals I first interacted with. As time would have it, I too became a teacher and I am forever proud of the profession.

Mr. Simba led a very simple life and was devoted to his work. He hailed from Kemera in Kitutu Masaba and operated from his home which was a fairly long distance away from Kenyenya. However, this never deterred him from reporting for duty as early as seven in the morning. In fact, we always found him in school despite the fact that his home was farther than ours. Parents who stayed in the church encampment provided him with lunch before he returned home.

One day, something strange happened; nobody brought him food. For the first time, I discovered that just like any other human being, Mr. Simba could get angry. He sent pupils to inquire from the parents what was amiss. The parents responded and promptly brought him the food.

Teaching is a noble profession. I believe, unlike any other profession, teaching has the most impact on young people. This happens because the teacher provides direction to the child when it is away from home. In fact, I regard teachers as secondary parents. Personally, I see it as a critical role bestowed upon teachers by God. Teachers spend a lot of time with learners and this is why they should carry themselves diligently so that they play their rightful roles as models and the light of the society.

Mr. Simba played this role very well. He taught us handwriting reading and reciting numbers vowels and the English alphabet. Gradually, I could read and write words in Ekegusii which was the language of moderation and instruction in class. At the time, we used slates as exercise books and a special chalk-like stone as pencil.

Recently, Kenya introduced a new curriculum of education to replace the 8-4-4 which was introduced during President Daniel Arap Moi's tenure in 1984. The new system, dubbed the Competence Based Curriculum (CBC) excites me. It is expected to be a game changer in the country. Its architects say that it will ensure that children are assisted to identify their potential and fall in the right careers and competencies.

To me, CBC rings another bell in my mind. It reminds me that I sat for the Common Entrance Examination (CEE). The term 'competence' is a common denominator in the CBC and the KACC. However, I will not go on to compare and contrast the two. When I sat for the examination and excelled, I qualified to join Motagara Intermediate School. The school is near my late mother's childhood home.

At the time, learners at Standard Four sat for the KACC. Once they qualified, they proceeded to Standard Five. This was the starting level for intermediate school, Motagara in my case. In the earlier years of studying, I had gone through Sub-Standard A and B which was equivalent to Standard One and Two. After Sub-Standard B, I proceeded to Standard One, Two, then Three, marking the end of primary education. Basically therefore Standards Five and Six were like Form One and Two.

Generally, very few children from my area attended school. The norm was that many children spent their time looking after their parents' livestock and assisting in the farms. Schools were situated very far apart. For example, Motagara was centrally placed to attract learners from as far as Gesima, Esani, Nyagachi and Kenyenya. In total, the school had slightly over two hundred pupils. Depending on the time they accepted to join school, some looked older than others. However, this did not deter them from competing fairly in studies as study mates.

My mother Atalia Nyachoke

My father, Gatimel Gisore (Arieri) next to my car

My father's 3rd wife, Nyanchama

Mama Kemuma my father's 2nd wife; 2018

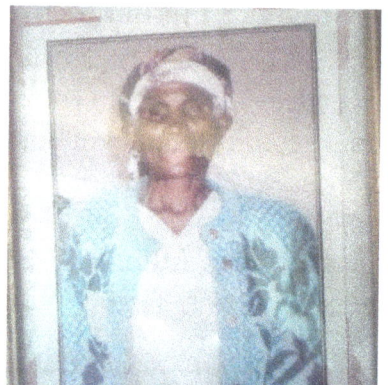
Motondo, my father's 4th wife

With Mama Kemuma Arieri (seated left) Mrs Anari, MrsTariki from Bobembe & my wife Elizabeth

Arieri and Matundura

My aunt Nyang'ate

Moturi and Nyang'ate

My uncle Bonyi

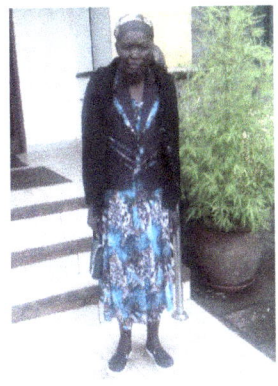
My sister Miriam Onsongo

My mother-in-law Yunuke Bina Nyakang'o

Patriarch Arieri (centre) with sons visiting me at Mecheo

With my brothers visiting Mama Kemuma Arieri
before she passed away in 2019

My first house at Nyabisimba, built in 1960

A section of Nyabisimba Area

Part of Nyamira County

A tarmac road through my Nyabisimba home area

Some members of my extended family at Riamabea SDA Church at Nyabisimba

Some members of my extended family members in Nyabisimba

# From Boy to Man

In Gusii, it was mandatory for boys to make a date with the circumciser's knife. This was a major way of transitioning from boys to men. Circumcision was critical, for it marked the departure from childhood and the start of adulthood. Traditionally, the community had clear, strict and intricate rituals to be followed to the letter, from preparation of the initiates, subjection to the circumciser's knife and other ceremonies thereafter. It was believed that going contrary to the laid down procedure was an abomination that would spell a curse on the family. For example, the people believed that it could bring impotence on their sons, unless the affected family offered sacrifices to appease the ancestors.

My parents took a different view. Having been baptised and having resolved to stick to Christian teachings and values, it was not easy for them to make a number of decisions that contravened the dictates of tradition. Some of the procedures that encompassed traditional circumcision were in direct conflict with their Christian religious beliefs. For instance, at church, they had been taught against partaking traditional brews like *busaa,* yet this was a major component of partying and merry-making in the community especially during ceremonies like circumcision and other major events. Christians had also been discouraged from making sacrifices to the gods, for the Bible was clear to them that there was only one Supreme Being.

> Christians had been taught that a man would not light a lamp and put it under the bed but on a raised point so that all can enjoy the brightness. In December 1954, my parents as well as a handful of their fellow converts whose sons were my age agreed to walk the talk by coming together to ensure that our circumcision did not follow the traditional script as laid out. These age mates included Elkanah Omanwa, Ben Osoro and Zephaniah Motaroki. Since the church encampment idea at Kenyenya had been wound up but the huts were intact,

our parents organized for us to be circumcised and be accommodated in one of the huts for a number of days. The period of seclusion would be sufficient for us to heal.

Traditional circumcision as it were was never a walk in the park. The traditional surgical procedure was painful but worth it. It needed one to be courageous and able to withstand the pain. Shedding a tear was regarded a sign of cowardice and would bring disrepute to the initiate and his family. Once the circumciser was done with us, he led the youths who had accompanied us in singing this song (*esimbore*[1]), which was the signature tune of circumcision ceremonies.

*Oooyo! Oooyo...eee (Here he is, here is!)\*2*

*Omoisia omoke 'mbororo bwamorire (he's experiencing pain)*

*Arwane bobisa (Let him battle the enemies)*

*Otureirwe ritimo (His spear has been sharpened)*

*Arwane Sugusu (Fight in the North)*

*Arwane Irianyi (Fight in the South)*

*Arwane Mocha (Fight in the East)Arwane Bosongo (Fight in the West)*

*Moisia nyake Bororo bwamorire (The boy is in pain)*

The song simply announces that a boy has graduated into adulthood. It also confirms that he endured the pain and was ready to tackle any challenges in life with great pride and courage.

We stayed in seclusion for over three weeks, doing nothing other than playing, sharing stories and being fed. At the end of the period, our parents organized a ceremony where they invited neighbours for a feast. However, the feasting was devoid of traditional brews, dance and other utterances that were seen to contradict the church doctrine.

---

1  Editor's Note: In **The Gusii of Kenya: Social, Economic, Cultural, Political & Judicial Perspectives (Nsemia Inc. 2017),** *J. S. Akama offers has a comprehensive discussion on the rite of passage and the implications of this rite on the initiates and the community.*

# Scaling the Heights

I vividly remember my first day in Motagara Intermediate School in 1952. When I entered the compound that morning, I saw two boys engaged in a fistfight. I had seen such a physical confrontation before in my former school but I did not expect such a scene to welcome me in my new school. It was actually one of those playground things that attracted cheers and jeers from onlookers.

As I soon gathered, the two boys had bumped into each other over a stolen ball. The ball, improvised from nylon bags and threads was one of the major assets a school boy owned. The clash triggered fighting between the two boys. One punched the other in the face and blood oozed from the nose.

"Stop it," a pupil who was fairly older said as he ran in to separate the two boys. "You are here to become gentlemen and not bullies. Change your grumpy ways." The message was intended for the two boys but I got it too, and I promised myself to ensure that I live by it.

Motagara Intermediate School was centrally placed. It attracted learners from a wide catchment area as alluded to earlier. Some came from as far as Nyakongo and Mochenwa in the present day Kitutu Masaba constituency and Nyaramba in Borabu Parliamentary electoral area. Despite the distance, all learners were day scholars. This comforted me that, although my home was about five kilometres to the school, it was fairly near.

It was not common for Mr. Webster who was the Inspector of Schools to visit our school. However, whenever he did, pupils got excited as teachers busied themselves than never before. For learners, the presence of the Briton swaggering along the tuition block excited us because of obvious reasons; it was not every day that we spotted a white man in and around our place. We wished to get closer to him and even shake hands with him but our teachers could not allow us. Whenever we overheard him speak to the teachers, we never comprehended what he was saying. We just giggled as we turned our faces away, lest we attract unwarranted wrath of the teachers.

I noted earlier that a teacher touches the life of his students directly. In my view, this is the major reason as to why teachers should strive to impact positively on the children. They have been entrusted this noble task of imparting knowledge, skills and competencies in the younger generation. When they get it right, their names forever get stuck in the learners' minds.

From my experiences in Motagara Intermediate School, I remember two teachers who outshone the rest in touching and shaping my life. One of them was William Buruchara who later became a pastor in the Adventist Church. He has since died. I loved the way he dedicated himself to give us the best training and I looked forward to excel in his subjects. For instance, whenever he taught us about the Bible (later called Christian Religious Education), he told us stories from the good book and contextualized them very well to our lives. This made me think that he should have pursued Theology. And as if in answer to my thinking, he eventually pursued the course and became a pastor.

It is not uncommon for pupils or students to give nicknames to some of their teachers. These nicknames come as a result of a teacher's manner of dressing, walking style, body size or shape, his speech and general behaviour. The situation was not any different during my days of study at Motagara Intermediate School. We nicknamed one of our teachers Mr. Singapore because he loved mentioning the name and with a unique tone. The name seemed to go in line with his deep voice, stern looking eyes and posture. Whenever he walked while swinging a cane in the hand, it appeared that he was a tough man who should have served in the military. The nickname became so popular to the extent that it veiled his real name.

Away from studies, I was very active in Physical Training, later renamed Physical Education. Due to my exemplary display in this field, teachers would occasionally task me to train my colleague pupils in the field. This went a long way to improve our general fitness. I was also good in athletics and could represent the school during the location competitions in the mile and half mile events. These competitions were often held at Sironga, where schools including Sironga, Motagara and Kebabe would assemble. The events attracted several spectators, including parents.

Time flew fast at Motagara Intermediate School. After four years at the school, I sat for the Kenya African Preliminary Examinations (KAPE) in Standard Seven and posted impressive marks. The good results secured me a place at the Government African School (GAS)-Kisii in 1958. The Government African School, Kisii, was later named Kisii School. It has since grown to become a national school.

There was excitement and anxiety when the results were announced. At the time, it took a couple of days for a candidate to know his or her particular result. When I got mine at the school, I was very happy. My parents were equally happy as were people from our area. This was a milestone for me, considering that the school dropout rate was very high at the time. Many dropped out because their parents could not afford fees to keep them in school. Others were simply not motivated!

I was lucky because my father was a trader engaged in livestock business. He also grew maize, pyrethrum and other crops. Apart from this, he had a quarry from whence he could excavate murram and building stones that he sold. Some of these building materials were bought by people who built semi-permanent houses at Kebirigo market. The money he got enabled him to pay my fees and meet other financial obligations for the family.

The power of religion in transforming one's life at the time was also evidently manifest in my father. Although he never acquired formal education, he chose to be the pioneer parent in embracing formal education. Indeed, he was among the few parents who took their children to school. Apart from him being a born again Christian, my father worked closely with Dishon Nyabuga. Nyabuga who mainly did timber business had travelled to various parts of the country and seen the kind of life other Kenyans led. He is credited with introducing new crops like tea in our area. He was also the first person to introduce wattle trees. Above all, he rooted for other income generating activities like trade, and my father was his good student on this.

Fate works in its own ways. I joined the Government African School, Kisii, at a time when it offered secondary school education and, at the same time, served as a teacher training centre. Mr. Gerald, a Briton, served as the overall principal. When we stood in the assembly on my first day at the school, I realised that I was the tiniest and probably the youngest of the boys in the school. However, two teachers (Ogonji and Odhiambo) must have seen it differently or they had other interests which overshadowed what they saw. These two teachers, who hailed from Luo Nyanza, recommended that I was too old to be in a secondary school classroom. To advance their own formed and concluded opinion, they recommended that I skip the school and join the teacher training section. This move did not affect me alone. My colleagues John Ongaga and Mweresa Orare were also picked out. However, I did not have a platform to protest or someone to turn to as much as I wished to do so.

I have to emphasize that this rudimentary decision did not augur well with me. I had a desire to get secondary education because, in mind, it would enhance future opportunities for me. If I excelled in secondary school examinations, I would proceed to university and pursue a career of my choice.

Oddly though, I had not come across anyone who had obtained university education. Worse yet, at Motagara, we never had career or motivation talks that would give us pointers to the future. However, from history lessons and reports through the radio, I had read and heard about people who had obtained formal education. These people had gone ahead to serve in the colonial government. Key among them was the Tom Mboya. I imagined that if I completed my education, I would equally become a successful and focal (or even vocal) person. With the setback at Government African

School, Kisii, I wondered that joining the teacher training college was going to limit me to teaching. Although I admired teaching, I had not made up my mind to pursue it as a career.

Nevertheless, and with no other option at hand for us, Ongaga, Mweresa and I reluctantly accepted to be moved to the teacher training section.

But, there was a bigger problem! The government had decided to close down the teacher training section in GAS, Kisii. Students in that section were required to transfer to Kabianga Teachers' Training College (site of present-day University of Kabianga) in present-day Kericho County.

I noted earlier that at the time, Kericho was in Nyanza Province. Kisii fell under South Kavirondo District. The former Nyanza region had four districts namely; Nyanza South, Central Nyanza, Kericho and North Nyanza. Later, North Nyanza became Western Province while Kericho was hived off to form part of the Rift Valley Province.

In Kisii, Paul Mbuya was the clerk of the African District Council. He stayed in Nyanchwa on the outskirts of Kisii Town. However, due to politics, some members of the Gusii community demanded that the boundaries of South Nyanza be reviewed. Their intention was to have Abagusii separated administratively from their Luo neighbours. When this happened, Homa Bay and Migori remained in South Nyanza while Gusii region was given its own district, then called Kisii.

I remember that during competitions in intermediate schools, Kericho competed with South Nyanza at Tengecha and Gusii Stadiums. Then, senior chiefs Musa Nyandusi and Tengecha turned up to cheer their respective teams. At the time, and for many years on, Kisii did well in athletics. I do not understand how the athletics tides changed in favour of Rift Valley. However, I feel that leaders from Gusii region should go back to the drawing and help the community revive the sport.

At Kabianga Teachers Training Centre, there were several students. They included seven and three from the Luo and Gusii communities, respectively. The institution was headed by a European, one Mr. Popkin. There were also eight tutors of African origin. They included Nelson Moguku who handled Woodwork and Carpentry lessons. From Moguku, I left the institution well-versed in carpentry and woodwork. Some of the furniture I made due to the skills I obtained from him is still in my home to this day.

Despite its status, the institution was not connected to electricity. Instead, we used pressure lamps at night both in the classrooms and hostels. As we acclimatized ourselves to the college environment, it became clear to us that although Mr. Popkin was a foreigner, he had a soft spot for Kalenjin students and disfavoured those of us who hailed from Gusii and Luo Nyanza. This prevailing scenario ignited bad blood between the Kalenjin students (who were the majority largely using the fact that the college was located within their community) against the Kisii and Luo.

As days went by, the animosity worsened. There were clear lines between the 'natives' and the 'outsiders', with the Kisii and Luos sharing a hostel while the Kalenjin resided in another. Additionally, in our hostel we had a defective pressure lamp that would go off suddenly, a situation that would force us to finish the chores at hand in darkness or sleep and wait for dawn. This often angered us. Our persistent call to the administration to fix the problem once and for all often hit a dead end.

It was against this backdrop that we decided to take the law into our hands and vent our anger on our Kalenjin colleagues who seemed to laugh and ridicule us each time our lamp went off. On the fateful evening, we threw our lamp away and forcefully took theirs. This did not amuse them and there was push and shove that culminated in a chaotic scene. We overpowered them and they vanished from the compound as we sung victory songs.

When Mr. Popkin got the report the following morning and came in to address the matter, we felt that he was evidently biased from the onset. When we dug the matter up to establish the origin of his favour for the Kalenjin, we got wind that his wife was initially barren. This bothered the couple, until a time when a Nandi herbalist gave his wife some concoction that eventually healed her and she started bearing children. With this family problem solved, Mr. Popkin seemed to believe that he owed the Kalenjin community allegiance and favour at every step.

*****

Mr. Popkin who initially served as a military officer in the colonial administration was literally running the college as a personal property. From our perspective, his leadership style spoke volumes about his incompetence. We just looked forward to the time we would complete our studies at the college without a major incident. It was thus a big relief for us when Mr. James Mbotela came in as one of the tutors. But for Mr. Popkin, he appeared unsettled. Mr. Mbotela had served in Shanzu Teachers College and made it shine over other colleges in the country. He had also authored a book, *Uhuru Wa Watumwa,* which was very popular with students. Mbotela was the father of celebrated journalist, Leonard Mambo Mbotela.

Under Senior Mbotela's tutelage, Kabianga was elevated from a teacher training centre and renamed Kabianga Teachers' Training College. We were elated! We walked with our noses in the air when we wore shirts with the new name of the college emblazoned on our chest pockets.

The Mbotela phenomenon spread fast in the college. He was an authority in education management and administration. It appeared that whenever he spoke, Mr. Popkin never objected. Mr. Mbotela was a role model for us to emulate. His wife worked as a District Development Officer and was friendly to students and tutors alike. However, some European women dreaded her. Perhaps they wondered how fast she got an education and a colonial government job.

In Chinua Achebe's book of our times, *Things Fall Apart,* Okonkwo comments about Nwoye thus, 'a chick that will grow into a cock can be spotted the very day it hatches.' When

I retrospectively relate this quote to nationally acclaimed journalist Leonard Mambo Mbotela's early life, I feel that I should have instinctively told his father that his son would one day become a broadcaster.

Leonard was a fast playing and cheeky little boy. I had become friends with his father and he told me to occasionally get to his house and teach young Leonard basic skills like counting, writing and reciting the alphabet. Leonard could stand on the table and start singing when we least expected. Perhaps he did it innocently as any little boy would, but his actions created a lovely, entertaining atmosphere in the house.

*****

When time for teaching practice came, a language barrier stood between many trainee teachers and pupils in the neighbouring schools. Ordinarily, most trainee teachers hailed from the Kipsigis communities around the college and easily interacted with learners whenever they went out for teaching practice. This was not the case for those of us who came from other communities.

To this day, primary school trainee teachers of the non-Kalenjin origin go for teaching practice in schools around their college. This makes it easier for them to operate from their college on a daily basis without incurring overly high costs. Mr. Mbotela thought that this arrangement disadvantaged some of us. Through his intervention, trainee teachers were posted to Sironga, Nyangoge and Kebabe Primary Schools in Nyamira. I was first attached to Sironga and later to Nyangoge Primary Schools during my internship sessions. The two schools offered me an opportunity to get well-grounded in teaching.

When I stepped into a classroom as a teacher trainee for the first time, I was very excited and equally perturbed. I was excited because I knew that soon, I would graduate as a teacher and be able to impart knowledge as a full time teacher. But at the back of my mind, I wondered how my teaching would pan out, given that I was a young person, almost the same age as some of the learners at Sironga Primary School.

Our tutors could visit the schools for inspection and individual assessment. During such times, one could tense as the tutor sat in class and followed the lesson. Personally, I was never afraid of the tutors. I believed that they had passed through the same stage and excelled. Further, I believed in myself. I knew I was well grounded in all subjects as was required of a primary school teacher.

I was glad when I excelled in the final college examinations and was posted to my former school, Motagara Intermediate School in 1959. When I reported to my former school now as a teacher, I looked at it as a great honour bestowed upon me by God. At the time, my favourite teacher Buruchara had left the institution. Interestingly though, I got good company there in the names of Nelson Akuma and Daniel Osoro. They were vibrant, ambitious and focused to deliver as teachers.

# The Love of My Life

In today's world, some parents encourage their sons to marry once they are through with their college education. The parents tend to think that at this stage, the sons are mature enough and can effectively take care of their wives and establish their own families. This was not the case especially in the pre-independent Kenya. Then, parents gave their sons' marriage prominence over college education.

When I finished my studies at the intermediate school level and excelled in the Kenya African Preliminary Examinations (KAPE), I was approached with a suggestion that I was ripe to take in a spouse and start my own family. Indeed, my sister who follows me had been married off. Our in-laws promptly paid the dowry in form of cattle. According to Abagusii customs and practices, these cattle were supposed to transit to another home in exchange of a young girl who would come in to be my wife.

This arrangement disadvantaged the girl child. Although my sister Mary was younger than me, she had been married off (at 16 years of age) to Onsongo Bogonko of Mosobeti in Kitutu Masaba. At the time, girl child education was not a priority for many families or the community. Truly, nobody would blame my parents for marrying off my sister before I married. Her matrimonial home is not far from ours and her new home was acceptable to my family.

I did not object to my father's idea of getting married. However, I did not have any girl in mind suitable for me to marry. This was not strange of me. Unlike now, back in the day, it was not a young man's task to search for a lady and propose to marry her. Marriage was a highly valued communal affair and was treated as sacred[1].

Parents paid special attention to the arrangement of identifying a lady who would become their daughter-in-

---

1    Editor's Note: for a detailed step-by-step Gusii traditional marriage process see Daniel Momanyi Mokaya's **Enyangi y'Ebitinge (Nsemia Inc., 2020)**

law. Then, they identified and tasked *esigani* (sponsor/go-between) the onerous responsibility of gathering intelligence on the girl's character, upbringing and family background. This special person *(esigani)* had to be someone trusted by the parents.

For my case, my aunt Nyang'ate, my father's sister, was given this task. She was already an adult married to Nyangoge area and who would be trusted to make a decision that would not disappoint the family. This is the intricate procedure that culminated in the identification of a beautiful and well-behaved lady who eventually became my wife. Her name is Elizabeth and her childhood home is in Bonyamatuta, not very far from where I was born. After the pre-marriage procedures, which included dowry negotiations, the deal was sealed.

It is interesting that, although I was an active youth in the church just as my wife was, we had never seen each other. I saw her for the first time during a ceremony called *ekerorano* which was part of the marriage arrangements. *Ekerorano* preceded dowry payment and I doubt if one would have even dared reverse the arrangements for perhaps disliking the would-be spouse.

We paid ten heads of cattle as dowry and soon walked down the aisle in Nyangoge SDA Church in 1957. The wedding was attended by relatives, friends and curious members of the community. I was happy because I had walked in the footsteps of my parents who married through a Christian church wedding some years earlier. This is why I chose to start this book with their marriage because this is where my story is premised. My father and mother form the foundation upon which I came into being.

I believe that marriage is a heavenly union. However, in modern times, materialism and other factors have watered down the institution of marriage to a big extent. When I got married, I only owned a grass-thatched house. Most of the wedding attendees walked from their homes to the church. We did not have any resources to spend extravagantly but we had one of the most memorable weddings. It was officiated by Pastor Nathaniel Nyanusi who was then stationed at the Nyanchwa SDA Conference headquarters. Save for the rickety luggage lorry that gave my wife and me a free lift from Kebirigo market to our home after the weeding, we did not have any other vehicle.

I noted there above that when I got married, I only had one grass thatched house. At that time, I did not know that God would open his floodgates of blessings to bless us. God had His plans for us and the plans were good.

After I became a teacher, I marshalled savings and built a house with a roof made of iron sheets. It was the first such house, not only in my home area, but in the environs too. Until the time I roofed it, neighbours did not know what was in my mind and what the house was going to look like. They were only worried of its notably big size. When the roof shone with sparkling iron sheets, people came from far and wide to witness the new phenomenon.

They were amazed further when I brought in masons who plastered the walls and cemented the floor. This made the people say that a *mzungu's* house had been built in their community. The house monumentally stands to date on the plot I inherited from my father and I value it because it is part of my history. My first two children were born, breastfed and weaned in that house. I intend to renovate the house. It will then remain to be a constant reminder to my nuclear family and my descendants, showing them how God has been good to me.

My wife and children

My first & second born children: Zablon Agwata & Jane Mabea

My wife and I attending graduation of Zablon in 1981

My wife and I attending graduation of Zablon in 1981

During my son Zablon's wedding

During my son Mong'are's wedding

During my son Geoffrey Aori's wedding

Aori and his children Jim &Jones at Leeds University

Joyce Aori and Petronilla at Leeds university

Aori's wife with Jones &Jim at Leeds University

I'm standing 3rd right with my eldest son Zablon (2nd left) & other family members

With my wife Elizabeth at home

My wife Elizabeth at home

My family at Zablon's home

I am with my Son Benard, his family & my wife

My grandchildren at my home

With my wife & daughters Jane, Carolyne, Irene and Alice

A section of Borabu Settlement Scheme

My home in Mecheo

With Mrs Grace Nyakomarere Fay & Mrs Teresia Gichuki (my korera)

When Dr Mical Kado (my korera) visited us at home

One of the sites I visited in Israel

One of the sites I visited during
the Israel trip

# 2. MY CAREER IN TEACHING

# My First Posting

Watching the kind of life our teachers led and the insurmountable respect they commanded, I felt that being employed was a wonderful thing. Teachers' children were equally lucky, for they hardly lacked whatever they needed. Teachers appeared to lead happy families, something that ignited a sense of admiration in me. I looked forward to the day I would get a job and earn regular income like those teachers I so much admired.

Particularly, I envisioned that formal employment would give me a chance to network and prepare myself for the real world. Additionally, and this was more important to me, it would open floodgates for my own money. As the first born in our family and as I grew, I did not like it whenever need prompted me to ask for monetary help from my parents. I wanted to get my own money and be able to support them in uplifting the living standards of our family.

I started the journey of my career on a rainy morning. The rain had reduced to slanting showers, then to sprinkles when I stepped out of the house. The light from the overcast sky had been diffused but the clouds indicated that there would be more rain.

When I reported to Motagara Intermediate School, I was happily received by learners and teachers alike. Daniel Osoro, the headmaster, was glad to receive me and boastfully so. He told the pupils that I had studied at the school some years earlier and now returned there as a teacher. The school had about ten teachers, and nearly all of them were older than me, save for John Ongaga who joined the institution the same time I did. Ongaga had been my college mate and was my age as well. He was soon transferred to Sironga Primary School. In my early days at the school, I operated from home. But after some months, I was allocated a house within the school compound. This was the norm at the time.

The school had not changed much since my days as a pupil. Indeed, the number of classrooms had not increased. However, they had gotten older. That said, the school now had over three hundred pupils compared to the two hundred or so during my time as a pupil. There were fewer girls than boys, largely because girl child education had not taken its rightful place in the hearts of the parents. Learners who excelled in examinations would either proceed to secondary school or be absorbed into the teaching profession as Untrained Teachers (UTs).

As required of a primary school teacher, I did not cling to teaching particular subjects. However, I was delighted when I was allowed to teach in upper primary classes. And, for my entire teaching period, I never taught lower classes.

My appointment letter posting me to my former school Motagara Intermediate School had my starting salary as Sh350 per month. This may sound a financial joke today but it was a huge amount of money in 1959. At the time, Sh350 would have easily enabled me to buy five cows or several goats. It would also buy me several suits and household goods.

I was over the moon when I received my first pay. Earlier, I had not owned any amount of money close to Sh350! The amount was substantially reasonable for a young man who had not earned a salary before. I gladly bought myself a suit and a pair of shoes as I saved the remaining amount for other projects, including the purchase of a bicycle that would ease my mobility.

Unlike now when the powers to hire, discipline, fire and retire teachers are vested on the Teachers' Service Commission (TSC), at the time, I was hired by the Local Authority of Kisii, what later became the Gusii County Council. The TSC would be established much later.

The Chinese say, "after you is good manners". I was good mannered when I was a pupil at school. I left the school with a good grade and a good name in 1956 when I sat and passed in the Kenya African Preliminary Examinations (KAPE) that was administered in schools under the colony and protectorate of Kenya. Therefore, this assurance made me report to the school once again with air of confidence, not as a pupil but as a teacher. The situation would have been different if my name had made it to the list of truants and culprits in the institution.

I was young and energetic and I desired to become the best teacher. I was devoted from the word go and ensured that I endeared myself to the learners. My favourite subjects were Geography, History, Mathematics and English.

I also loved creative activities, especially sports and scouting. In the school, I was instrumental in establishing and maintaining the vibrancy of the Scouts' Movement. I was motivated into these activities because I had actively participated in sports all along, especially while at Kabianga Teachers College. Due to the special attention and passion I gave to the scouts, the club magnetically pulled pupils to join. It did not take long before the management of the school loved and embraced the club as it played a central role in moulding lively learners and making them embrace discipline.

The beauty of teaching is that one develops a photographic memory over time. This enables one to master the names of his students. It therefore goes without saying that even as I advance in age, I recall a good number of my students by name. For instance, athletics legend, the late Naftal Temu, was one of my pupils at the school. At the time, he was a tiny slender boy. When I saw him, I at once told myself that with his athletic figure, he had a lot of potential. Indeed, during Physical Education lessons, Temu exhibited a rich athletic talent. I resolved to invest in training and nurturing him alongside other pupils in athletics.

At the time, sports were not a very rewarding career for pupils. This made it difficult for many teachers to put much emphasis in such activities. However, for me, I believed that sports were ideal for body fitness and fun. Above all, when I looked at pupils like Temu, I saw a rich long term potential in him. He only needed an opportunity to unravel this latent potential. For instance, however young he was, he joined the track each time I trained older pupils. In most cases, they would finish ahead of Temu and I could encourage spectators to cheer him until he finished the race.

Once in a year, we held 'locational sports' that had a variety of competitions, including athletics, ball games and cycling. For Bogirango schools, the locational sports were mainly held at Sironga or Nyamaiya grounds. These fields are still being used to date. However, I feel that they should be elevated from mere playgrounds to stadia. I have to salute Kisii County Government for elevating the status of Gusii Stadium. The facility often played host during district competitions. Due to the massive facelift, it now has a VIP pavilion, a smooth play surface with underground irrigating system, among other features. This will encourage more sports enthusiasts and tap talent at the grassroots.

*****

I have also to note that I was among the first people from my area and its environs to complete studies and get a job. Unlike today, there were very few teachers. I was regarded highly, although some children could either take off or admire me from a distance. It was a near abomination for a pupil to remain seated whenever a teacher passed near him. This did not mean that I was fierce. In reality, the children did not have any better way of showing respect to their teachers.

Any teacher will tell you that his love for the job hits a crescendo when his pupils succeed. It is for this reason that, at a personal level, I was happy when Naftal Temu became a national figure. He won a gold medal in the 10,000m at the inaugural 1968 Summer Olympics in Mexico. During the event, Temu led an African sweep in the men's race, beating Ethiopia's Mamo Wolde.

The World Athletics wrote this when Temu died in 2003:

> "Wolde took the initiative at the bell and held on to the lead until the last 50m, at which point Temu fought his way past to win Kenya's first ever gold medal, after a last lap of 57.4."

Temu was equally good in half marathon.

These exploits in the track made Temu become a household name in Kenya. President Jomo Kenyatta awarded him with a piece of land in Borabu Settlement Scheme for making our country proud. I was very sad when he died in 2003.

A teacher's satisfaction and happiness are rooted in the success of his students. During my days at Motagara, learners performed well in the Kenya African Primary Education (KAPE) examinations. Those who did well at the time include Prof. Benjamin Ondigi and Pastor Stanley Onchaga whom I taught History that formed part of the General Paper. Their success in examinations reinforced my resolve that I was in the teaching profession to stay.

I occasionally receive calls from some of my former pupils who are now serving humanity in various capacities across the world. Others have already retired. That is the beauty of teaching; the teacher-pupil bond never breaks, more especially when the latter succeeds in life. The situation is different when one's students fail in life. Such people may see you from far and vanish into the bush.

*****

I noted above that my starting salary was Sh350. Today, this amount cannot buy you much. But back in the day, this was a good pay. However, I have come to understand that no one will ever have enough money. Each day, man is looking for money and, indeed, more money. Those who have a lot of it are the most aggressive in the search for more wealth. Perhaps one can only be at peace if he gets satisfied with what he already has even as he pursues more to replenish it.

My opinion is that the best thing one can ever do is living within his/her means. I lived within my earnings, albeit with a little straining because I was the only salaried family member and in formal employment at the time. Apart from meeting the family's day to day needs, I was able to make savings. Through the savings, I managed to build an iron sheet roofed house.

Since I was among the first people from our area to get an education and a job, I became a role model and reference point. People who were also salaried were very few. They included Joseph Osero Nyaberi who at the time worked as a clerk at

Gusii County Council. In 1966 he was elected to parliament in a by election following the demise of Thomas Mong'are Masaki. He became the first MP for West Mugirango after the electoral area was hived off from the larger North Mugirango Constituency.

Parents would encourage their children to work hard in school so that they too would get money to build descent houses in future. I was happy when young people came to me, seeking advice and guidance. Over time, they were able to study and get jobs too.

As presented elsewhere, apart from building the unique house, I was able to buy myself a brand-new bicycle. Owning such means of mobility then was a milestone in upward trajectory. The bicycle eased my movement between my home and my place of work, although I spent most of my time at school because teachers were provided with accommodation within the school.

For many years, teachers have held the mantle as the light of their communities, in particular, and society, in general. Apart from imparting knowledge to learners and moulding them to become responsible citizens, teachers hold key positions in the society they live in. Some become politicians while others make politicians. Still others become pioneers and leaders of life changing groups and organizations. Teachers in my days established trends that later became the norm in their communities.

**Biographer's Note:** Mzee Stephen Mabea's pupils speak excitingly about him. For instance, Retired Pastor Thomas Onchagwa of Nyamira Seventh Day Adventist (SDA) Conference spoke at a funeral of Mabea's relative and said that he was Mabea' pupil at Motagara Intermediate School. He said thus:

> "He taught us History. Due to his mode of presentation, I easily understood the lessons and some of them are stuck in my mind to this date. For example, I remember how he painted a candid picture of Scottish missionary and physician David Livingstone's exploration of Africa, a sojourn which began in 1841. He explained how David Livingstone, who is credited

to have made a contribution towards the discovery of earlier medications against malaria among other diseases, openly spoke against African slavery. Indeed, through my teacher's presentation, I learnt that by the time David Livingstone died, he had positioned himself as a staunch abolitionist of slavery who believed in the dignity of Africans."

*****

During my youthful days, I held various responsibilities away from school. For example, I was the founder member and the brain behind Keboye Welfare Club in 1959. In the preliminary stages, I consulted closely with like-minded people like Joseph Osero Nyaberi. At those initial stages, many did not see the need of the group and they ignored us. But within a short time, they saw sense in us coming together and supported the initiative. The group brought or sought to bring together members of Abagichora clan. It was our desire to have the clan united and empowered through business and politics. Particularly, we needed to get empowered economically. We envisioned that this could be achieved faster if we pooled our thoughts and ideas together, especially with respect to farming and trade. For instance, through this unity, we were able to establish Nyabomite and Nyangoko coffee societies in West Mugirango. I held the position of Treasurer in the club for many years.

One may wonder why the group comprised of Abagichora only during its formation. One may also ask why we did not loop in other clans from the constituency.

Perhaps I should answer this by saying that, at the time, it was largely assumed that one was safer depending on how closer he was to his clansmen. Specifically, it was easier to trust one's clansmen than anyone else. Indeed, although clans relate in other ways including intermarriages, it was felt that those from 'in-law' clans would not be counted on in protecting our collective interests. So, Keboye was very specific: its members were limited to Abagichora clan and her related clans like Abakiambori, Abamanyanya and Abanyaiguba. These clans do not intermarry and have the same lineage. However, in 1969, Abamabacho were incorporated into Keboye, becoming a formidable force in terms of membership in the process.

I need to be clear that from onset, the group was meant to be apolitical. However, it will be illogical to deny the fact that it got infiltrated by politicians and politics over time. This infiltration was not a bad idea. The clan wanted to have a say on the political arena. We found the welfare group ideal as a platform upon which we could bring forth our preferred political positions.

Prior to independence, we had just one North Mugirango Location, as captured in the records of the colonial administration. The name Mugirango is actually a corruption of Bogirango. At the time, Borabu was part of the White Highlands and rangeland for the colonialists. Then, around 1964 in the lead up to the republic, Bogirango (Mugirango) was subdivided into two locations – North and West Mugirango. Later, following the dissolution of the Senate in 1966, both North and West Mugirango became constituencies with Borabu incorporated into North Mugirango. Only much latter, in 2013, did Borabu become a constituency of its own.

When West Mugirango became a constituency of its own in 1966, we worked day and night using the Keboye Welfare Group network for Joseph Osero Nyaberi to become our pioneer Member of Parliament. Coincidentally, Thomas Mong'are who was the MP for North Mugirango had died in a road accident in 1965, occasioning the by-election.

When Mong'are died, the entire North Mugirango constituency was shaken. He had been propelled to the national limelight due to his eloquence and charisma in articulating issues that afflicted the people. Indeed, nothing illustrates the fact that Mong'are was a popular leader, and possibly destined for a bright future had death not snatched him, other than the fact that he was named after hundreds of children. In fact, I am one of the parents who proudly named a son after this great leader of the time.

Mong'are hailed from Bonyamatuta clan and so was Senator John Kebaso who represented the whole of Kisii in the Senate. There was a feeling in some quarters that Abanyamatuta (those of Bonyamatuta clan) were enjoying a bigger share of government and political positions. Indeed, apart from Mong'are and Kebaso at the helm of politics, Ochieng'i Kimoro who served after being elected as Bogirango Chief as provided by the law then, equally hailed from Bonyamatuta clan. Further, the homes of these three leaders were not far apart. Literally, power resided in proximity within their clan. This brought forth disquiet as the other clans felt left out.

When the by-election was called, it did not cross Joseph Osero Nyaberi's mind that he needed to contest. In fact, Mong'are's death, the split of the constituency to North and West Mugirango and the eventual declaration of the by-election caught us flat footed. Although we wanted to have representation, we did not have someone from our clan in mind who should enter the political ring. As likeminded opinion shapers within Keboye, we mobilised our thoughts and settled on Osero. He was at the time an employee of Kisii County Council.

We were racing against time and we thought that Osero would jump to the idea once we approached him. However, when we did, he said he had not made up his mind to risk resigning from the council to run for a political seat. This appeared to be a drawback but we stuck to our guns, assuring Osero that we had solidified our people and would all throw our support behind him. Even as we persuaded him, we crossed our fingers. If he adamantly refused, the scenario would likely plunge us into shame. This is what we feared most. It would mark a false start for Keboye, an outfit that we had built for the good of our people.

When Osero softened his heart and made up his mind, we were happy. Members of the welfare were asked to whip their relatives into supporting our candidate, Osero. Luck played into our hands quite literally, as his name clicked with the voters with ease.

On Election Day, I had mixed feelings in my heart. Although I was almost certain that Osero's match to Parliament was unstoppable, some part of my mind told me that in politics, anything could happen. Even so, I kept praying and hoping for the best. True to my prayers, our people heeded to the call and overwhelmingly supported Osero. At the end of the day, he was declared the winner! Among the candidates that lost in the election was Chief Ochieng'i Kimoro who had resigned from his position to contest.

Victory is sweet but victory in an election is sweeter. When Osero was declared the winner, a celebratory wave swept through the breadth and width of Keboye territories and beyond. The pronouncement was made at Manga and immediately, the celebrations reverberated through Isecha, Bonyunyu, Nyamira, Nyamaiya, Kebirigo and other areas as a motorcade escorting the newly elected MP to thank the people traversed the constituency.

As the dust settled following Osero's win, clans associated to Keboye realised that their unity was worth it. As the group officials, we literally had the guts to emphasize that for the people to thrive, they had to speak with a common voice on communal matters. Due to the influence Keboye wielded, we were able to lobby for other key positions. For instance, Stephen Ongoro became the chief, easily succeeding Kimoro, and beating candidates like Victor Kebaso (from Bonyamatuta and a nephew of John Kebaso) and Nyangoro (from Bosamaro).

For many years that followed, politicians used Keboye to raise their profiles, beat their opponents politically and ascend to power. Thomas Mong'are Masaki, Joseph Osero Nyaberi, George Morara, retired Judge David Onyancha, Sospeter Mageto, Dr James Gesami and Henry Obwocha are some of the politicians who won or lost their parliamentary seats, depending on how they played their cards with or against Keboye.

Some politicians who knew that I was one of the architects of Keboye would come to me for advice from time to time.

Some used the advice to win while others ended up failing miserably. Presently, the Keboye approach may not be effective. In my view, it is an idea whose time has elapsed. For it to work it will need a new approach for the Abagichora clan to retrace their steps and get united once again but while taking into account and appreciating that political power is transitory.

In reality, the welfare aspect of Keboye collapsed a long time ago. Part of the reasons as to why it collapsed was that it reached a time when its leadership did not have day-to-day contact with those at the grassroots. For instance, I moved to Borabu Settlement Scheme. Other co-founders and supporters also moved or have since passed away. Keboye may not have achieved much of what informed its formation, but I treasure its achievements. I am proud of having been part of its architects.

*****

In the 1960s and 1970s, most farming in Kisii focused on various crops, among them pyrethrum. The plants, with blue-green leaves, white flowers with yellow centres grew from numerous fairly rigid stems. Healthy pyrethrum grows to 45-100 centimetres. They are economically important as a natural source of insecticides. In the Kenya highlands, pyrethrum was introduced by the Europeans settlers.

The introduction of pyrethrum in Kisii is credited to former Kitutu chief, Zachary Angwenyi and my uncle Dishon Nyabuga. Due to his administrative network, Chief Angwenyi easily influenced his people to embrace the crop at a time it fetched meaningful returns. Closer to my home, the crop was introduced by my uncle Nyabuga, a man who, despite the fact that he was not formally schooled, had travelled widely, doing business, learning best agricultural practices out there and coming home to implement them.

Previously, most parents could not afford taking their children to school because they could not afford it. Indeed, the money economy introduced by the colonial administration was taking a toll on the people who did not have a source for gainful income. When pyrethrum was introduced, many embraced growing it, due to the fact that the government was supporting the initiative and the crop flourished quickly. With its introduction, people started earning good money and could take their children to school and meet other family financial obligations. The history of the Kisii Community cannot therefore be delinked from pyrethrum and more so those of us who were of age at the time.

Apart from teaching and holding the position of treasurer at Keboye Welfare Group, I also played an instrumental role in the promotion of pyrethrum farming in my area in the 1960s. This is when the global insecticides industry was vibrant and relied on pyrethrin, an extract from the pyrethrum plant. Those engaging in pyrethrum farming earned good returns. This enabled many parents to educate their children from the crop's proceeds. With these good returns many were also able to invest in other income generating activities like retail shops.

Through my uncle Nyabuga's initiatives, farmers in our area got training from field extension officers. They were able to understand the potential of the crop and know its proper husbandry practices. They thus made bumper harvest and got good earnings.

I was among the first people to embrace pyrethrum farming. At the time, the government was also promoting the formation of cooperatives. The cooperative movement envisioned pooling resources in order to realize effective and efficient marketing of farm produce. Aside from pyrethrum cooperatives, there was coffee and dairy farming.

I was one of the members of the Kerina Farmers' Cooperative Society. Since I could read, write and speak effectively in English and Kiswahili, I was elected to become the treasurer of the society. This society was based at Kenyenya where we built its offices. The buildings are still intact, next to Kenyenya dispensary. Other pioneer workers in the society included Nehemiah Mariera who was the secretary and Johnson Makori who rose to assume the position of Manager at Masaba Farmers Union. The latter had officers at Keroka and its buildings are intact as well.

Since Kerina Farmers' Cooperative Society was affiliated to Masaba Farmers Union, I was lucky to be elected to represent the union at the Regional Pyrethrum Board of Kenya. However, I later vacated the position when I moved to Mecheo in Borabu Settlement Scheme.

Members of any family that engaged in pyrethrum farming hold everlasting and nostalgic memories of the crop. The most strenuous part of pyrethrum farming was picking the flowers. Since they grow to knee height, adults and even adolescents would only harvest them on bended backs, for several hours. Some parents tasked their children to harvest the crop too as the young ones were more agile.

The harvested flowers would be dried in the sun at home, then packed in gunny bags and delivered to the pyrethrum societies. At the society stores, a clerk weighed and recorded a farmer's deliveries and issued a receipt. Farmers were paid for the crop at the end of the month.

Each season, every society was given a target. If they did not meet the required number of kilos, they would miss out in terms of handsome earnings. At the time, the sector was closely monitored because pyrethrum was a major cash crop and foreign exchange earner for the country. I cannot recall the exact number of tonnes that we harvested in a season. However, I recall that farmers were very happy with the venture. Through Masaba Cooperative Union that had affiliate societies from Bobasi, Bogirango, Nyaribari and Bogetutu and under the able stewardship of Dishon Nyabuga as Chairman, we left a mark that should be indelible in the history of our people. However, since many of these stories are undocumented, the upcoming generations may not fathom and appreciate the journey those before them traveled. This is one of the reasons as to why, in my small way, I have told my story in form of this book.

Although the sector later collapsed, we managed to purchase a plot in Kisii Town. We developed the plot. Our building at the plot was named after the union. It was among the modest buildings in the town at the time and stands to this day. Each year, I get some earnings in form of dividends from the project through the union.

The pyrethrum industry became a major employer in the country. Nakuru Town where the Pyrethrum Board of Kenya (PBK) was headquartered became a household name amongst Kenyans.

However, I should state that the decision to locate the PBK headquarters in Nakuru did not go unchallenged. Indeed, there had been earlier plans to establish the factory in Kisii. Those in support of this idea argued that Kisii was the major source of the crop. They missed out, albeit with discontent. They were disgruntled and claimed that the decision to deny Kisii the factory was politically instigated. It was rumoured that although Nakuru was not the major producer of pyrethrum, then President Jomo Kenyatta pushed for the establishment of the factory there, ostensibly to use it as bait that would stimulate growing of the crop in areas such as Molo and Nyandarua that were closer to his home tuff, Central Kenya. Although we read this as sinister and oppressive against Omogusii, and protested in equal measure, the government had its way. This of course increased costs of transporting our harvest to Nakuru but we had to live with it.

The late Henry Onyancha Obwocha was among people from Nyamira who got employed at the PBK. An outstanding accountant, he rose to the position of Chief Accountant of PBK. He would later plunge into the turbulent waters of elective politics. He was elected to represent West Mugirango constituency for three uninterrupted terms, and served as a minister in the government of President Mwai Kibaki.

Of all things, I never imagined that the pyrethrum industry would collapse. Kenyan pyrethrum enjoyed a good market internationally. However, just as it happens in many other public sectors, the pyrethrum industry was infiltrated by workers who did not have the interest of the famers at heart. These workers would embezzle farmers' resources unashamedly. Coupled with a cutthroat competition at the international market, the local industry found itself on a stiff cliff. It slid to the rock bottom, at the detriment of the economy of individual farmers and the country. Additionally, part of the reason for collapse was what happened in the global market with the creation of synthetic insecticides that were massively produced and were cheaper than pyrethrum derived ones. At the time, environmental concerns were not at the level they are today considering that the synthetic products harm the environment more than the naturally produced pyrethrum-derived products.

This is part of what Prof Peter Ndege who teaches History at Moi University wrote about pyrethrum in an article published in the Daily Nation on January 24, 2020:

> "Exports of pyrethrum extracts continued to increase in subsequent years before declining phenomenally since the 1990s.
>
> "The main reason for this decline was that the pyrethrum subsector became a victim of many challenges, which also bedevilled the rest of the agricultural industry.
>
> "First were the delayed payments to producers due to PBK's inefficiency. Second were the deteriorating terms of Kenya's external trade, which led to deficits in the country's balance of trade and payments.
>
> "Other challenges included poor infrastructure and extension services; expensive inputs, including high fertiliser costs; continued use of outdated technology and climate change.
>
> "As a consequence, most smallholder peasants exited pyrethrum growing to engage in the production of better-paying alternatives like Irish potatoes, onions, tomatoes and vegetables.
>
> "Consequently, production of pyrethrum, the protector of people and other plants against attack by pests, has declined inexorably, with little being done to restore the lost glory."

When the sector collapsed, assets which belonged to farmers were gradually vandalized. Parents who had leapt out of poverty found themselves drawn into it once again. They could not afford to pay fees for their children nor afford basic family necessities. Some of the children had to abandon their studies midway. The collapse of the industry shuttered dreams of many.

In Nyamira and Kisii, you can still find the deserted pyrethrum cooperative societies in places like Motagara, Nyagachi, Nyabite, Kebirigo and Sironga. They stand on plots which have since been grabbed or encroached on. In some areas, the plots have been converted for other uses of public interest. Still in the two counties, residents, especially those who are my age, will tell you that they used proceeds from pyrethrum to make a major difference in their lives. Apart from educating their children, they build better homes composed of semi-permanent houses. Still others purchased pieces of land at newly-created trading centres and established business premises there.

According to field extension officers, in the sector's good days, Kisii produced the best pyrethrum. Interestingly, when I look around, I find that not every farmer discarded the crop. It appears that some still have a very intimate attachment to the crop despite the bottlenecks confronting the sector. Indeed, some farmers in areas like Nyaribari Masaba, Nyaribari Chache and Bobasi constituencies spared it in their farms. However, the production is low. They sell the harvests to agents at throwaway prices.

I have previously heard that the County Government of Kisii has intentions of reviving the sector. The idea sounds good and I support it. However, my worry is, due to intensified subdivision of land due to our archaic inheritance practices, the venture may not be economically sound for some families. Apart from subdivision of land, the soils have become overused. Crop rotation is not practised in many homes now because of diminished land sizes. Crops like maize, which is the stable food in Gusii, are now doing very poorly. Unless action is taken now, I am afraid our people are potential candidates for relief food in the coming years. It is high time our people diversified their diets, more especially at a time like now when our stable food is doing poorly due to land overuse and recurrent cases of diseases like maize necrosis.

The fall of the once stable pyrethrum industry should serve as a lesson to everybody, and especially our young people. The industry failed in part because of mismanagement caused by individuals whom farmers placed total trust on. These individuals let the farmers down and caused the suffering of many. I believe that when one gets entrusted with leadership especially in business, he should offer the best service possible. It is the only way that one can leave a good legacy on exit. Unfortunately, it appears that people no longer care about legacies as was the case in the past.

The tragedy that befell the pyrethrum industry did not spare the coffee sector. It is an open secret that coffee that was once a major cash crop from Gusii has no more allure. There are ominous signs in the tea sector! It is struggling and could be headed the same way, as the other two, unless stakeholders candidly discuss and agree to fix the bottlenecks facing the sector, once and for all. I am happy that Peter Munya who is the Cabinet Secretary for Agriculture is determined to reform the ailing sector. This will particularly benefit the small tea scale grower.

## Aborted Trip

It has been argued that high expectations make frustrated men. But as elucidated by playwright John Ruganda in *The Burdens,* one can argue that equally, little or no ambition cannot take you far. I grew up an ambitious young person. Moderate ambition, I should say.

In the early 1960s, Kenya was at the verge of attaining self-rule. At the time, the colonial government rarely allowed Kenyan students to travel abroad for further studies. But deep in my heart, I was convinced that if I managed to get out of the country, I could land on better opportunities. Indeed, Kenyans like Romano Kiome and Lawrence Sagini had studied abroad and had been thrust into public life as soon as they returned to the country. In Kisii, Sagini became a house-hold name.

It was against this backdrop that a number of young men made attempts to get out of the country in 1959, albeit illegally. I hatched such a plan with my close friend and former college mate Hezbon Mweresa who hailed from Kiabonyoru area in the present-day Borabu Constituency. In the plan, we sought the help of friends to assist us with safe passage, so that we could seek greener pastures in the Union of Soviet Socialist Republics (USSR, also referred to as the Soviet Union), Russia or any of the republics in the Union.

We had learnt from James Mbotela, our tutor at Kabianga TTC, that it was possible to get out of Kenya through the Indian Ocean. These escapes usually happened when schools closed for holidays. We were determined to try our luck. However, because this was an illegal undertaking, we had to keep the plans as close to our hearts as possible.

In retrospect, it feels rather crazy that I left home without informing any member of my family, including my wife. No one would have actually suspected that we were up to such a sojourn because, as I left home, I did not carry any personal effects or academic documents. I knew that if I shared this information with my family, nobody would have accepted to let me go. I therefore told myself that I would only inform them of my whereabouts when I got to or near my destination.

When Mweresa and I got to Mombasa, we planned to take a boat which people informed us belonged to the Coast region's kingpin, Shariff Nassir. The journey was to start from Malindi. As such, from Mombasa to Malindi both of us were locked in a large tank that had little ventilation, save for tiny openings at nose height. The tank would then be hauled on a boat. At the start of the journey to Malindi, we were served with two loaves of bread each, to silence the pangs of hunger during the trip. When I look back, I doubt that this journey was worth undertaking.

We did not fully consider the risks that were involved. In reality, we risked being hauled into prison in a foreign land. Psychologically, this unexplained silence would have tortured our families for months if not years. We could also be faced with hunger since we did not have sufficient money to buy food for the unknown number of days of the journey. Further, we did not have prior arrangements on who would host us at the destination, nor did we budget for accommodation once we got to the foreign country. In fact, we did not have a particular country in mind that would be our destination. What a risk!

Because our travel was against the law, we had to hold it as a top secret even at the harbour in Mombasa. Indeed, we had to pose as regular people as possible. We did not want to offer any hint that we were strangers and our intentions were to get out Kenya.

We had done due diligence and had been informed that the discomfort in the tanks would not last long after leaving the harbour. Those who shared the information with us said that the tanks would be opened after we left the shores and covered at least ten miles on the Indian Ocean that then belonged to the British Empire Zone.

We got to Malindi safely and boarded the boat that was headed to some foreign country. When the boat got off the shores, excitement swept through my heart in the hope that, finally, my dream would materialize.

However, my excitement was short-lived. After covering about seven miles in the waters, the boat developed complications. Our lives were now in overhanging danger. To save our lives, it was decided that the boat should return to the harbour. Those who wanted to travel would be allowed to do so in a week's time.

I was disheartened. I had not set aside any money for emergencies such as the one we were in. So, when we left Malindi and travelled by road to Mombasa, I knew that my troubles had just started. Unlike my friend Mweresa who had some little extra cash with him to travel home in case the journey abroad aborted, my pockets were empty. Worse yet, the money my friend had was not sufficient for bus fare to get the two of us back home. Inevitably, we parted ways. It was one of the most painful scenes anyone can imagine.

Mweresa travelled back home while I remained at the coastal city of Mombasa. Here, I had to find a way to survive. Even so, I did not want to spend a lot of time looking for a decent job because there was none waiting for me. I had to take any work that came along first. This is how I landed myself at a construction site where I was allowed to join other young men in sinking a foundation for a building.

Due to the way I dressed which was fairly modest and the manner in which I engaged my co-workers, two of them were able to learn from me that I was a teacher who had driven himself into trouble in pursuit of a dream. Word about me also reached the late Jaramogi Oginga Odinga who was reportedly one of the contractors. When we met, Odinga was in the company of Sharif Nassir. They were touched by my plight. The two raised some money for my journey home, so that I could retrace the bearing for my life that was almost going into ruins. The train journey from Mombasa to Londiani in the present-day Nakuru County lasted almost twenty four hours. However, it appeared that when I connected to Kebirigo (then called Maeri) using a bus, the journey got even longer and I spent a full day on it. Today, this journey between Londiani and Kebirigo takes three hours or less using public road transport.

Once at Kebirigo, some wave of excitement hit my heart, for I was now not far from home. I bought some fruits and hurried homewards, on foot. As I narrowed the distance, I told myself that I would not divulge details of what had transpired during my aborted trip. Instead, I made up a story to the effect that I had abruptly travelled to Kisii for work-related issues and was not able to reach the family.

My wife, siblings and parents happily received me. My absence from home had caused them a lot of anxiety and left them unable to decide whether to let it known to everyone that I had gone missing or wait until I resurfaced. Fortunately, they bought my cooked up story and did not have many questions for me. It was after a couple of years that I frankly revealed to them what had transpired. They were astonished.

*****

Once home, it did not take long before I reconnected with Mweresa. We were glad to meet once again. After extensive deliberations, we resolved to give the aborted sojourn another attempt. This time we would use a different route.

Some people we interacted with in Mombasa, who were privy to escape routes from Kenya, had advised us to cross the border to Uganda. At the time, Uganda was a British Protectorate while Kenya was a colony. From Kampala in Uganda, we would take a flight to Khartoum, in the Sudan. These tipsters told us that a Ugandan by the name Wandegeya would host us in Kampala. Once in Khartoum, the same person would help us navigate to Addis Ababa (Ethiopia) via road, before we could take a flight overseas.

Travelling was not an expensive affair at the time. With a month's salary of Sh350, one could travel to Uganda, stay for a couple of days and return home without financial strain. So, after we received our wages, we embarked on our journey to Uganda. As usual, we held the move close to our hearts. For me, I never shared this critical information with anyone in my family, including my wife. I merely told her that I would be away for a couple of days. Funnily again, she never asked me for more details even if she would have wished to. I had two children at the time (Zablon and Jane) and they were quite young to notice that I was set for a long journey.

This was an illegal venture, just as the first one. Therefore, I did not need to make elaborate preparations. On the material day, I only carried a few of my clothes in a bag. I also carried my identity card that was at the time issued by the Kenya colony. We got to Uganda after two days on the road and were happily received by Wandegeya who showed us around and hosted us.

One may wonder why a wedded man who had gotten a good education and acquired a teaching job was undertaking such risks that may not appear worthwhile at face value. Well, in the late 1950s and early 1960s, joining Makerere University was the big thing. A few people had studied or secured a chance to study at Makerere. It was the only university college (and later university) in East Africa. Those Kenyans who walked in the corridors of Makerere were big news in Kenya. For instance, Lawrence Sagini was a household name in Kisii, having been among the first people to study at the institution. However, for me, my chance to join the institution was literally quashed at Government African School, Kisii, where some teachers alleged that I was too old to be in the secondary school track. So, I thought that I was not meant to pursue that part and did not have interest to do so.

Apart from becoming a Makererian, getting a job as a clerk in the colonial government was big news, just as teaching was. However, the spirit of adventure was telling me a different thing. It was telling me that there were greater opportunities outside East Africa. I was determined to satisfy this yearning by succeeding in going overseas, just as my cousin Momanyi had done.

Mweresa and I were probably headed into trouble and were taking too long to learn. Our first trip had aborted and this particular one was not showing any signs for a breakthrough. In Uganda's capital Kampala, the plan was that we enter one of the old cars that were carried in a big truck. Some of the cars were to be destroyed at the truck's destination while others could be repaired. This travel arrangement appeared workable in our favour but it was not readily available and we had to wait. It turned out to be a long wait!

With nothing else to do in Kampala, we grew impatient and anxious from day one, unsure of what could befall us if our plans were scuttled. We had become acquaintances with Wandegeya but as days passed, our hopes got blurred. They dimmed altogether in a week's time.

One night, following our week's stay in Kampala, I lay in bed and sleep eluded me. I tossed around in bed almost all night, turning one way and then the other. I blankly stared at the ceiling, and soon fell into a meditative mood about my life. I recalled the journey I had travelled thus far. I recollected that my parents had given me a good education. I was their first-born child and they had banked their hopes in me to steer my siblings to prosperity. Then I pondered on the fruitless attempts, first through Mombasa and now Kampala. I had made an attempt to flee my motherland yet nobody had attempted to eject me.

Taking all this into consideration, I could not understand why I was being this ambitious, let alone putting my life in danger. What about the teaching job I was leaving in Kenya? What of my young family? What would they do or how would they cope without me? 'If I want to live long enough to see my children grow up, and play with my grandchildren and great grandchildren, then I must abandon this idea of leaving Kenya,' I finally told myself.

I shared this with Mweresa the following day, with an intention of prevailing upon him to join me on my journey back home. However, it appeared that he was not about to make up his mind. Clearly, I could tell that he was not convinced with my narrative. He appeared more resilient than I was and could stay longer. I therefore wished him well with whatever lay ahead of him and made my journey back home.

By the time my friend Mweresa threw in the towel, I had reached home and readjusted to the life. I had come to terms that journeying abroad for me was work in futility. I had decided to concentrate on teaching and being a family man.

As I later learnt from Mweresa, he had run short of finances while in Kampala and could not afford bus fare for the trip back home. Being a man, he could not sit and cry for help that was not in sight. That is how he got a teaching job at a secondary school on the outskirts of Kampala, although he was not qualified for it. He was trained to teach in primary school just like me. Later, he made an attempt to cross to Ethiopia on foot but got lost and ended up in a forest in the Congo. He wandered for several days before some Tanzanians transporting timber from the forest found him. He was disturbed, dejected and frail. The Tanzanians must have pitied him and offered to rescue him. They travelled in the same vehicle to Tanzania, where he got hospitalized. When he recovered, he started his journey back to Kenya, a sojourn that lasted him a better part of a week.

By the time my friend Mweresa made it home to share his harrowing experiences with me about twelve years later, I was the headmaster of Kisii Primary School. I had totally put the dream of ever stepping out of Kenya for further studies behind me. I was now fully focused on teaching and shaping pupils' future. I think in retrospect, that I had made a wise decision. I now believed that I was more useful in my country. Although my kinsmen say that 'no road tells one what is ahead', I would have probably wasted myself out there.

*****

I noted earlier that Mweresa and I were neither the first nor the last young Kenyans to attempt their luck elsewhere in the world. My cousin Momanyi Moturi (he would later acquire a medical degree) had successfully made it to Russia in the Soviet Union, then a communist country. We had seen each other grow to become young adults and the distance between Kenya and Russia was not about to cut the bond.

Unlike today, communication at the time was mainly through letters. Such letters took weeks, or even months, to reach the intended recipient.

One time, Momanyi sent me a letter when I was still at Motagara Intermediate School. It was held for several days at the post office in Kisii Town. This happened because it bore stamps of its source, a communist state and it was unimaginable then that the recipient could be in as remote a place as Nyamira.

The matter must have appeared shocking and overwhelming to the Post Master. This prompted him to request the services of a police inspector, a British colonial officer, to deliver the letter to my school. The officer's arrival caused panic and excitement at the school. While teachers wondered what brought the officer to school, the learners, many of whom who had never seen a white man got excited.

Before the officer handed the letter to me, he spent several minutes interrogating me. He said he had been dispatched with the letter to the school to establish the kind of person I was and why I was communicating with people living in a communist state. I did not know where this conversation was headed, but I remained calm and told him that the author of the letter was my cousin. Further, I added, I did not know where he was stationed since he left home without disclosing his intended destination.

The officer appeared to have come to give me a dress down. He had already gone through the letter and established that Momanyi had insulted the colonial government in Kenya. With bitterness in his tone, the policeman read the letter to me, posing at every sentence, and sometimes explaining the way he understood its contents. When he drew to a close, he looked at me straight in the eye and said, "never, ever correspond with this man!" I assured him that I would not do so. In any case, I affirmed, I did not have my cousin's address.

When the officer calmed down, he gave me a pen and a paper and ordered me to write a reply to my cousin as he dictated words to me. At the end of the exercise, I had written a letter with a high voltage message, telling my cousin off for running away from Kenya and ridiculing the British Government. Having ascertained that I had abided by his instructions, the officer folded the letter into an envelope, which I addressed to my cousin. He then left with it for posting.

By the time the officer left my work station, I had sweat a lot. Further, I was disturbed that if the letter got to my cousin, he could doubt my sanity considering the terse words the colonial officer had made me use. Luckily, the officer had not realized that, although he had literally held me hostage, I had managed to see my cousin's letter that bore beautiful ball pen handwriting and quickly crammed the address.

As the ordeal ended, I resolved that I had to find a way of rescuing the cordial relationship I enjoyed with Momanyi if the letter I wrote under command of the policeman ever got to him. How was I going to do it? I wondered.

I recalled that, after I left Uganda, I had come with my friend Wandegeya's address. So, I resolved to write two letters: one to Wandegeya and another to Dr Momanyi. I would then put my cousin's letter in a smaller envelope, address it, then sandwich it in Wandegeya's letter. In Wandegeya's letter, I explained to him the precarious position I had been pushed into. I also gave him instructions to post Momanyi's letter. From then on, my cousin and I could communicate through the third party, Wandegeya. Momanyi would send me a letter through Wandegeya and I would reply through the same channel. This was in the understanding that Russia did not have any problem receiving letters from Uganda. Equally, there were no restrictions in sending letters between Kenya and Uganda.

I noted earlier that if luck had played into my hands, I too would have made it to Russia. Perhaps, once there, I would have managed to enhance my education. However, I believe this was God's intention and I do not have any regrets whatsoever on the turn of events.

Of course, I had not met anyone who had returned from overseas to share with me on experiences out there. For example, my cousin Momanyi returned home much later, having acquired a degree in Medicine. As soon as he came to Kenya, he was recruited in the Kenya Army (now the Kenya Defence Forces) as a cadet. He had an illustrious career in the public service and also invested in the health sector. One of the notable investments was Masaba Hospital in Nairobi.

Momanyi is now deceased but he left a legacy behind and the entire family is proud of him.

I have to state that Momanyi is just an example of those who illegally fled Kenya but came back empowered and more useful to the country. However, over time, illegal immigrants have had their fair share of trouble, including death during the sojourn, arrests by the police, drug abuse and deportation. When these things happen, they destroy one's life and it takes a fortune for someone to pick the pieces and find the bearing for his or her life.

I also noted that when Mweresa returned home, I was pleasantly surprised. It had taken about twelve years since our last contact. All along, I prayed for this miracle to happen for, quite literally, I was the last person from my community who was last seen with him. So, when he came to Kisii and I was called to the District Commissioner's Office to meet with my visitor, I was overjoyed to find that he was the one.

Life had not been fair to him. He looked much older for his age and I could see traces of disappointment in his face. However, his eyes beamed when they met mine, and I thought that I had rekindled his hope. Apparently, he had come to the District Commissioner to request for a permit to sell poultry in Kisii Town. At the time, such a job appeared demeaning for his level of training as a teacher.

Mweresa stayed with me for the next five days. During the stay, I discovered that he was partly confused and was telling stories that were not 'adding up'. He needed elaborate counselling which I offered him and he soon returned to his home at Kiabonyoru.

Once you desert duty in a government job like teaching, you lose it. This is exactly what had happened to Mweresa. We had trained together as teachers and were employed the same time. However, due to his long absence from duty, he had been relieved of the job. It was by sheer luck that he was reinstated months later and posted to a school in South Mugirango. Soon, he got married while at the school and stopped ever attempting, let alone imagining, leaving the country in search of what had turned out to be elusive greener pastures.

# A Move to Nyansiongo

When a strange disease attacked members of my young family in 1962, I was terrified to the bones. My wife Elizabeth was sick, just as I was, but my first born son Zablon and his follower Jane were worse. At that time, I was a teacher at Motagara Intermediate School. Zablon was barely three years old and Jane was suckling. I feared for my children's lives more than I did for ours, the parents. I think it happens that, ordinarily, when a child is sick, the parent wishes that, if it were possible, he or she would suffer in the minor's place. At the time, Jane was very young and she could not express herself fully for us to understand the extent of the pain caused by the sickness.

We got treatment in Kisii General Hospital (now Kisii Teaching and Referral Hospital, KTRH) and Kendu Mission Hospital to no avail. These hospitals were far from Motagara. Due to travel and treatment costs, I was really drained financially. At the same time, all of us grew scrawnier and weaker by the day. Evidently, we were very sick and the treatment we were getting was doing little to stop the suffering. Days turned into weeks as the sickness pitched tent in our bodies. This got my buddies, like Johnson Makori and Nehemiah Mariera alarmed. At the time, Makori served as the manager of Masaba Pyrethrum Farmers' Union while Mariera worked at the Kerina Cooperative Society.

The two organized for us to be evacuated to Litein Mission Hospital for further treatment. We were hospitalized for several days. Due to the distance between our home and the hospital, very few relatives managed to visit us. The visits gave us confidence that we were going to overcome the sickness. When you are sick and people visit you at the hospital, you feel stronger and see hope of recovering.

We were very thankful to the Lord when we were discharged from the hospital after a couple of weeks. However, we did not come back to Nyabisimba. Instead, we went straight to my work station, and settled in the house I was allocated by the school.

*****

At the time, the 'smell' of Kenya's freedom from the hands of colonialism was in the air. This was a critical moment for the country. Kenyans were about to write their history with indelible ink, by seizing the chance to rule themselves. However, the excitement was not going down well with several white settlers. It was clear that the foreign settlers were not going to be kicked out of Kenya. However, some of them could not visualize a situation where they would be led by Africans. So, they were secretly finding ways of disposing their properties so that they could return to their native countries.

The settlers were either interesting or selfish, although I believe it was more of the latter. The places they earmarked for their settlement were the best lands for farming. Their former settlements, dubbed White Highlands, are found in the most fertile parts of the country. The places have cool climate that are neither prone to malaria nor sleeping sickness. The settlements were not infested with mosquitoes or tsetse flies. These settlers also considered the terrain of the areas and the viability of the activities they intended to undertake such as mechanized farming and cattle ranching. I suspect that this explains why they were not attracted to some areas like the volatile Northern Kenya and lowlands around Lake Victoria.

In the Kisii region, the white settlers occupied what became Borabu Settlement Scheme, now within Nyamira County. Nyamira was hived off from Kisii, which was a colonial division at the time. Borabu borders Bomet, Narok and Kericho counties in the Rift Valley. Part of it also borders Kisii County. Despite the degradation, I believe that Borabu is still the most fertile area one can ever settle in Gusii region. The area sharply contrasts with other parts of Nyamira, in terms of acreage ownership. The land sizes in the scheme are much bigger compared to other parts of the county. Those who settled in Borabu bought the land from colonial settlers.

These buyers managed to transact through the Settlement Fund Trust (SFT) that was established as part of the independence negotiations. The SFT was designed to enable Africans acquire land previously occupied by the departing settlers. A buyer would pay a fraction of the value of the land and clear the balance over time. The transactions would be done on a 'willing buyer willing seller' basis.

Jameson Onsase, Barnabas Achoki and I formed a group, with the aim of pooling resources and jointly buying land in the Borabu scheme. After buying, we could subdivide the land amongst ourselves. Onsase was the Chairman of Kerina Cooperative Society while Achoki worked as a clerk at the African District Court in Gesima. We borrowed this idea of purchasing land as a group from three men from Bobasi constituency. The three who included the late Chief Matayo had raised the required figure to buy land along the Sotik-Keroka road.

Those who had gotten land through the Settlement Trust Fund were lucky. Their parcels were far from the scheme's border with Bomet, an area that was the epicentre of cattle theft. The ugly incidents of cattle theft proceeded until a few years ago when the government reigned in the vice.

For the three of us, we were not worried of getting land close to the border. Indeed, like for my case, I was familiar with ethnic tensions back at Nyabisimba area which is a few kilometres to the Nyamira-Kericho common border.

The transactions were happening quite fast. For example, in a few days, 54 people from other parts of Kisii were able to acquire land in Raitigo area within the larger Borabu settlement scheme.

The three of us, having raised Sh90,000, mounted a search for a suitable land to buy. Our first stop was at West Sotik (Mecheo). We got a European settler called Pedro who agreed to sell us his land after his friend Hilo rejected our payment proposal.

It was approaching the year 1963. Our independence as a country was now inevitable. Pendro appeared to be in a hurry to leave. He appeared to be one of those who did not want to see Kenya ruled by Africans and, if it happened, he did not want to be part of it. He was disposing the land at Sh180,000 and we were required to raise a third of the amount. We already had this amount. However, our excitement was short-lived. There were underworld claims that blacks were secretly dislodging the whites from the land. This compelled Pendro to refund us our down payment. This was very frustrating especially to me. I wanted to relocate to this part of the country as soon as possible. In my mind, I hoped that the change of the environment would work in favour of my family's health and overall wellbeing.

I noted earlier that the white settlers were not going to be flushed out of their abodes in the independent Kenya easily. Instead, they were required to, among other things, construct schools whence their labourers' children would study. So, I secretly scouted for a school where I could teach if I got lucky to acquire a piece of land in the scheme.

My scouting drove me into the hands of a European called Mackintosh who owned Narangai farm in the scheme. In the farm was a school by a similar name, Narangai Primary School, which was at its formative stages and had not been fully recognized by the government. Narangai was a Maasai name. I learnt from Mackintosh that he had little time in the country. He was keen on leaving so as to return to his motherland, Britain.

With this information, I went to the Africa District Council (ADC) office in Kisii and told the officer there that the closure of Narangai Primary School was eminent. I told him that if Mackintosh left, nobody would be able to support the school. This would provide an excuse for African parents not to take their children to school. I warned that the area was likely to be a rich ground for continued illiteracy if he did not find a way of rescuing the school.

The officer was excited. He keenly ceded ground for me to tell him more. Encouraged by his interest, I told him that Abagusii knew Narangai hill as Nyansiongo. I added that the government should change the name of the school from Narangai to Nyansiongo in the long run.

I left his office a happy and satisfied man. It did not take long before the school's name was changed as I had suggested. I was pleasantly surprised when I was posted to the school, as the headmaster in September, 1963. This happened despite the fact that I was a mcre classroom teacher at Motagara Intermediate School. I had not even served as a deputy headmaster. Ordinarily, one was promoted to deputy headship before he got promotion to headmaster.

I did not protest the move. Instead, I viewed it as an act of double blessings: I would have a chance to get land in the scheme and there was a chance of well-being for my family. I also interpreted it to mean that my employer had used some parameters to tell that I would be equal to the task bestowed upon me: leading the school.

When I broke the news to my father, he smiled and laughed until I saw his molar teeth. He told me that I should report to my new work station without any hesitation. My wife and children were equally excited of the news.

Lawrence Sese worked as an Assistant Chief for one of the sub-locations of Bogetutu location. At the time, he was among the very few residents who owned vehicles. His was an old pick-up whose sighting evoked excitement in the area. The few of us who were already salaried looked forward to buying such a locomotive to ease our mobility.

When Sese heard that I had been transferred to Narangai, he was genuinely happy. He understood the situation I had been in, occasioned by the sickness in my family. He also put himself in my shoes and understood that moving my family and our possessions (however little they were) was a herculean task. So, he offered to transport me in his vehicle.

As I bid goodbye to my school, members of the Scout's Club at Motaragara were not happy that I was leaving them behind.

However, they escorted me to my new station as reality sank in us all that we were parting ways due to my call of duty.

*****

Joy swept through my heart when I got to the new school. It was now my new working station. Above all, I was launching my career as an administrator in a learning institution. The school sat on a fairly expansive compound compared to my former station. It had classrooms made of brick walls, although the roofs were grass thatched. I told myself that I was young, energetic and brilliant and hence equal to the task ahead of me. I knew that these were strengths that would make me turn around the school and leave it better than I found it when time to leave came.

At the school, there were two men who worked as teachers. They were from the Kipsigis community and smoked tobacco all day long. They appeared unwilling to welcome me. It also appeared that they were semi-illiterate and did not want to work with me. I was perturbed when I told them to formally hand over to me and they ran away. I never saw them again. It did not take long before the White man sold the land.

The school compound sat on 30 acres of land. This was a project under the Permanent Improvement Supply (PS) regulation that the settlers were required to comply with. Later, stakeholders changed the name of the school to Nyansiongo DEB Primary School. Some traditional singers had composed a song in praise of the Nyansiongo hill. The song illustrated how the hill received abundant rain which fell on young men and disfigured their hair (*chinyenche*). I told them if we named the school Nyansiongo, it would carry the identity of the place forever. Indeed, the school stands to this day. Many learners have gone through the school and are serving this country in various capacities.

I noted earlier that my initial dream of owning a home in the settlement scheme aborted at the eleventh hour when Pendro refunded Onsase, Achoki and I the down payment we had made for his land. We did not lose hope, though. Instead, we sustained our search for an alternative seller.

Soon, we were lucky to find a serious seller. But as plans advanced, we were confronted with yet another unforeseeable challenge. Our friend Achoki had not married and, at the time, an unmarried person could not own land. This meant that Achoki could not be allowed to buy the land with his name as one of the buyers. We managed to navigate through this drawback by enlisting his father's help. We used the name Naftal Nyariki in place of Barnabas Achoki. This way, the land purchase transaction was sealed.

We were excited to have the land at last and subdivided it amongst the three of us. Most of it had not been cultivated before. It had several thick bushes and wild animals wandered freely. We named the area Mecheo because of the dominant tree species (*emecheo*) that littered and towered over the rest in the area. The name has remained to this day. Today, we have Mecheo Primary School, Mecheo SDA Secondary School and Mecheo SDA Church, among other institutions in the area. These institutions, as well as Mecheo market, are a light to the community around them.

The history of Nyansiongo is told from different perspectives. Some of the perspectives are largely inaccurate. However, since I was there from the beginning, I wish to set the record straight through this book in as far as I know them.

One thing that is little known to many people is that Mackintosh was not a trained teacher. This tells you that he was never the first headmaster of the school. When we settled in the school, his wife Barbra became very close to my family. She loved my daughter Jane very much. Barbra would take Jane to her house or walk and play with her. She admitted that I was a well-organized teacher too. Within a short time of settling on Mackintosh's farm, my daughter grew healthy even as she became very fond of Barbra.

Barbra was a teacher too. She worked at a European school in Maseno and whenever she came home, she brought gifts for my daughter Barbra and my wife Elizabeth. Due to the closeness between Barbra and Jane, they ended up sharing the name Barbra, though informally. To this date, my daughter's childhood acquaintances call her Barbra. Mackintosh and his wife Barbra are long dead but I have fond memories of the couple and our relationship. I remember them in good light, although we lost touch with each other after they left the place.

> **BIOGRAPHER'S NOTE:** *A visit to Nyansiongo DEB Primary School shows a different story. One cannot tell at once that this was the academic giant during Mabea's time. The first ever buildings established before independence are still in use. They include an academic block of four poorly lit classrooms. Buildings which once offered accommodation for pupils and teachers are still standing. However, their roofs are no longer grass thatched but made of iron sheets. Most of the other classrooms and office were built during Mabea's time. In the office, I found a Minute Book and the School Logbook from Mabea's time where Mabea documented major activities at the school. The books have never filled up, an indication that most of his successors never used them. In fact, the next entry in the log book following Mabea's exit in 1972 is in 1991. As well, teachers at the school feel that the men and women who studied there should return and give the institution a facelift befitting the performance record they left behind.*

# Revitalizing Nyansiongo

Just as Malcolm X said, I too believe that 'education is the passport to the future, for tomorrow belongs to those who prepare for it today.' I witnessed the power of education when I joined Nyansiongo DEB Primary School in 1963. There were ready office jobs for anyone who excelled in education, from the lowest level to the university.

I joined the school when its enrolment was very low. Most parents worked as labourers in farms owned by wealthy individuals. The importance of education had not sunk in for some parents. Others saw the value of education, but they were torn between investing in the education of their children and 'living a day at a time' considering the low wages their employment fetched. Lack of adequately trained teachers did not help either but negated the uptake of education in the area.

It is against this backdrop that I assumed and held the headship of the school. Some parents brought their children to lay their foundations in Standard One. A few others had children who were about to sit for the Kenya African Primary Education (KAPE) examinations. However, this latter group was ill-prepared to face the examinations and post impressive grades that would secure them better schools.

Together with my teaching staff, parents and other stakeholders, we agreed to burn the midnight oil to offer our best to the learners. We converted some servants' quarters into makeshift dormitories for the students. We also instructed the learners to be 'mini-day scholars'. They could study and spend their weekdays in school, then go to their respective homes on Fridays. Strictly, they were required to report back to school on Sundays by 4 pm to start the new week together. If one failed to observe this regulation, he or she was required to report to my office the following day (Monday), accompanied by the parent or guardian.

The school had two hundred students, from the lower classes to Standard Seven. Three quarters of them were boys, my son Zablon included, while the rest were girls. This was not unique to the school. It was the trend across the country as many parents had not prioritised education for girls. We had to continue wooing parents around the school to let their daughters have access to education at the institution. Gradually, they yielded to this appeal and the gap between boys' and girls' population narrowed substantially.

I had a team of nine dedicated teachers. The outstanding ones included Peter Osinde, William Nyamwange, Billiah Bogita and Agnes Momanyi. Working together with these four and the rest, we ensured that pupils were well grounded in discipline, spirituality and studies. We also received massive support from the school committee whose first chairman was David Moindi. As more people settled in the settlement scheme, there was change of membership in the committee to reflect their diversity. Later, Stephen Obwoge took over from Moindi.

In total, there were about fifteen labourers' houses in the school compound. We repurposed these, a move that made it easier to accommodate the majority of the teachers in the compound. They could then hold extra lessons in the evening and very early in the morning. During normal class hours, teachers concentrated on revision and showing the learners the applicability of the concepts learnt. In the extra evening and morning classes, they focused on covering gray areas they felt needed more attention. The houses in the school really eased our work. I say this because the area was largely bushy. The road network was very poor and there were very few public service vehicles. It would have been overly cumbersome and risky to have teachers and pupils rise up in the wee hours of the morning to be in school for studies as we had envisioned. This would have also ruled out evening classes.

It did not take long before teachers and parents started seeing the results of their hard work. Notably, Peter Osinde made pupils like Mathematics. On the whole, our school drastically improved its mean standard score and became a household name in Kisii District and beyond. In the region, Nyansiongo could only battle it out for the top slot in the national examinations with Mosocho Academy. The latter, which is located near Cardinal Otunga High School, Mosocho, had full boarding facilities unlike Nyansiongo. This did not worry me. I knew that, unlike our competitors who received the best pupils from other schools at Standard Four, we never did the same. On the whole, my school was doing well, but I did not jump to the rooftop to sing about it. I did not see the reason to do so because the results were speaking for the school.

I was in my office one morning when I looked through the window and saw a white Land Rover snake into the compound. Such vehicles were exclusively owned by the government at the time. I knew at once that it had government officials. When I got a clear view of the vehicle, I realized that there were three other vehicles behind it.

Ordinarily, such a motorcade would have made me freeze but it did not. My conscience was clear as I was running the school as it was required of me. This confidence was reinforced by the fact that the school's results in national examinations were exemplary.

The officials from the Provincial and District education offices were accompanied by Kisii County Council clerk, Paul Nyachieo. Also in the entourage was the Kenya National union of Teachers (KNUT) Kisii branch treasurer, Bosco Mboga. Just as they stepped out of the cars and contentiously walked around the compound, I knew that they were either mesmerized or excited to be in the school. True to my speculation, the Provincial Commissioner, who led the delegation, admitted that they expected to find a school with spectacular buildings located in a town. "I least expected to discover that this school is located in a bushy and remote area like this," he said.

After a familiarization and fact finding tour around the school, I assembled the teachers and pupils to be addressed by the guests. We quickly put together a hand written memorandum, detailing the successes and challenges the school faced. At the climax of the meeting, I requested the indulgence of the chief guest for one of the pupils to read the memorandum to them. He obliged.

When Sarah Angima stepped forward with the memorandum in her hand, I saw the guests whisper amongst themselves. Sarah was a little girl, but she walked and spoke with charming confidence. I was not in doubt that she would do a good job. True to my expectations, she did not disappoint from the word go.

Sarah projected her voice nicely. One of my eyes was fixed on her while the other was riveted on the chief guest. I wanted to be sure that he was keenly following the little girl's presentation. When she got to the last full stop and bowed her head in appreciation to the guests' keen attention, there was an ovation characterized with cheers, whistles and ululations.

"Are you sure this is your pupil," the Provincial Commissioner asked me.

"Yes sir."

"This is a wonderful job."

Just like the Provincial Commissioner, some of the other officers had doubts that Sarah was a pupil in the school. Some argued that, perhaps, she crammed the words in the memorandum and only came to parrot it. The officers who had earlier indicated that they were in a hurry changed the narrative. They now said that they were going to be in our school for some time to fully appreciate what we were doing. We could not object.

They resolved to take the Standard Seven pupils in groups and engage them in various conversations in English. Some walked with the pupils to the playing field, while others strolled along the tuition block. After some minutes, we converged once again. They admitted that the brilliance exhibited by Sarah could be seen in several other pupils.

I am forever proud of Sarah and her classmates. They excelled from the school and proceeded to various national and provincial secondary schools. Save for a few who have gone to rest, many of them feature in the list of who is who nationally and elsewhere in the world.

For instance, Sarah studied in India and has worked in various offices. Currently, she is the Kisii County Executive Committee Member in charge of Health. She has served in the portfolio since 2013 when James Ongwae assumed office as the county's pioneer governor. Sarah's colleagues from Nyansiongo include Prof. Justus Ogembo who is a professor of Anthropology in the United States, Peter Anching'a who is an accountant and Dr Shem Oyaro, a veterinary doctor. Others are Francis Rosana who is a retired accountant and Prof. Richard Nyamwange, an economist.

They usually call me. I feel they hold me in good esteem. I was devoted to shape their lives. I led my staff by example by ensuring that I was always present in school unless when inevitable situations arose. I also had supportive parents who wanted the best for their children and we delivered it.

> **Biographer's Note:** *Sarah (Angima) Omache who is presently serving as the County Executive Member for Health in Kisii County had this to say:*
>
> *"I was a tiny girl in Standard Five when Mr Mabea gave me an opportunity to read a short speech to the Provincial Commissioner's delegation. This happened in 1965 and it tells you that as early as that time, Mwalimu Mabea had seen potential not only in me but other girls and boys alike.*
>
> *"He mentored us. We always looked up to him for direction. He was a good time keeper and we all embraced this culture of time keeping. As a result of his commitment and leadership, the school did very well. This is why he was moved from the rural school to Kisii Primary School. He is a man I sincerely respect."*

# A selfless Teaching Staff

It has been said now and again that a school is as good or bad as the head teacher. This may not be true, to the extent that the headmaster ought to be a team player focused on steering his school to the pinnacle of success. The fact is that success of a school cannot be monopolised by the headmaster or any single stakeholder.

At Nyansiongo DEB Primary School, I led a very dedicated team of teachers. There was a wonderful spirit that gripped us all to pursue a common interest. Teachers who handled Standard Six and Seven agreed to stay in school to offer maximum support to the learners. Parents equally played along. We ate together and socialised during our free time. This bonding was the glue that made us match forward as a team.

It should be remembered that the school did not really have modern houses that were meant for teachers. We had converted some of the houses left behind by the white settler into teachers' residences. Some acted as dormitories for our pupils.

We ensured high level discipline. Time wasting was greatly abhorred. Spattan Nyong'a was one of my very dedicated teachers. He was a young man then but he chose to stay in the school compound to be close to his pupils. Although a teacher at primary school level was expected to be a jack of all trades, we internally encouraged specialization amongst ourselves. This was done with the understanding that each one of us had his or her strengths in particular subjects. For instance, I took a huge chunk of science classes while Nyong'a handled English and Mathematics. Later, he rose to teach in secondary schools including Kiabonyoru High School from whence he retired as principal some years back.

Nelson Mikuro was equally devoted in his job just as my deputy Peter Osinde who taught Mathematics. Since the school was not connected to electricity at the time, Osinde could wake up early enough, to ensure the pressure lamp is lit. By the time pupils got to class at 4.30 am, they always found that he had written several math questions on the black board for them to solve. He literally made it a culture for every pupil to love his subject.

> **BIOGRAPHER'S COMMENT:** *Nyong'a Obuba, now a retired high school principal, was part of the robust teaching staff at Nyansiongo DEB Primary School during Mzee Mabea's headship. He had the following to say of his former headmaster:*
>
> Nyansiongo DEB Primary School was famous for outstanding performance; we had good results from year to year. Mabea, our headmaster, loved his job and gave it his all. He was open, transparent, outgoing and focused. He ensured that all stakeholders knew how he utilized school funds. Due to this openness and accountability, there were no squabbles.
>
> Despite the fact that he was a busy man, by virtue of his position as headmaster, Mabea never skipped any of his lessons. In case he did, he found time to compensate the learners for the missed lesson. His character drew staff members to emulate him.
>
> He never missed school unless there were extreme situations and which he made known to us. We always knew his whereabouts. This strategy discouraged teachers from absenting themselves without justifiable reasons and permission.
>
> Most importantly, there was internal constructive competition. The time table and timing of lessons were followed to the second. No teacher wanted a colleague to 'eat' into his lesson.
>
> It is important to note that I was a P1 teacher while Mabea was a P2. In fact, prior to joining the school, I had briefly worked as the pioneer headmaster of Sironga Harambee School (now a national girls' high school).
>
> One would expect or doubt if I did not look down upon him as less qualified than myself. Far from it! I accorded him the respect he deserved as the CEO of the school. I believe that once someone is given responsibility over you, you are duty-bound to respect him, despite his age, level of education or any other parameter. If you cannot respect the individual, then you should respect the office.

Mabea taught science while I handled mathematics. All teachers gave their subjects their best shot. Our pupils have gone to great heights and they are many that have thus succeeded, such as the Controller of Budget, Dr. Margaret Nyakang'o who was very good in my subject, Mathematics.

I left Nyansiongo in 1971 for Wang'a Pala Secondary School, having worked with Mabea for two years. This happened after I sat for the Cambridge Higher School Certificate Examination as a private candidate and passed.

In 1973, I was made the Headmaster of Kiabonyoru High School where I served for over 20 years. I applied the leadership style I learnt from Mabea and this helped me steer the school to great heights, recording major successes in the process.

"I enjoyed working under Mabea. I was his deputy and he gave me an enabling environment to deliver in that capacity. His dedication was a trigger for internal competition. Most of our pupils have had successful careers."

# Selfless Pupils

It is long since I retired from teaching. It is even longer since I saw Sarah Angima, Prof. Justus Ogembo, Peter Anchinga, Dr. Julius Ogeto, Dr. Samwuel Ombengi, Dr. Charles Ongeri, Dr. Jason Mochache, Consolata Mocha, Prof. Jacobo Angima, and many other students who graduated from Nyansiongo DEB Primary School. In fact, it is over fifty years since I saw many of them. Some like Dr Oyaro Mong'are have since died. However, when I think about them, I remember that teaching is a privilege and a calling. I call it a privilege because teachers shape young people's minds and their futures. Indeed, a good teacher teaches while a great teacher inspires. It is not an easy task but it is fulfilling.

Throughout my teaching days, I discovered that each child is created uniquely. I also found out the importance of the different backgrounds children come from. These backgrounds can work for or against their dreams and aspirations. Some learners have the fighting spirit and can hardly give up even in the midst of abject poverty, animosity and other frustrations. One such pupil from my school was Justus Ogembo.

Ogembo came from a humble background. His father died when he was very young. He was brought up by his widowed mother but, at some stage, he was left in the hands of his half-brother, alongside his twin brother Nyambuti. Nyambuti has since passed on.

Raising the little fees required for Ogembo to be in school proved an uphill task. I really felt for him because he was a very brilliant young man. His favourite subject was Mathematics and he could teach his colleagues in class during remedial hours. He was a good singer too. Equally, his love for *obokano* (an eight stringed Abagusii traditional instrument – a harp) was an open secret to anybody who knew him.

Due to his brilliance, a big heart and willingness to assist his colleagues do well in Mathematics, Ogembo was a popular name in school. Pupils loved him and equally pitied him due to the challenges he faced from home. Whenever he was sent home for school fees, the pupils got worried.

One night, Ogembo and his classmates sneaked out of school. They accompanied Ogembo to a farm where he had been contracted secretly to weed for fruit trees so that he could raise some money towards his fees. When I received the news of children sneaking out of school the following morning, I was taken aback. Why would pupils sneak out of school? I was not amused. In my mind, I thought that the pupils must have been up to some mischief and I needed to go any length to unearth it. However, when I inquired, I learnt that they had gone to assist their classmate finish the weeding contract quickly and be in school the following day. They told me that Ogembo was their unofficial Mathematics teacher and added that they wanted him to be in school so that they could maintain their Mean Standard Score (MSS).

Well, they may have committed a mistake by taking French leave from school. However, when I looked at it critically from a humanitarian eye, I thought that the end justified the cause. I was touched and moved by their gesture. I believe that this was an act of love that I am yet to come across ever again.

Luck was on Ogembo's side. When he sat for the Kenya Preliminary Examinations (KPE), he scored good grades and was selected to join Kisii School. I followed him to the new school and pleaded with the administration to be lenient with him as regards to payment of school fees. The administration agreed and waived the fees. They were very happy with Ogembo because he was good in class and in extra curricula activities, especially music. At the school, he composed several traditional songs which he sung in accompaniment of *obokano*. This endeared him to teachers and students alike. He proved me right when he excelled in his Form Four examinations. After $4^{th}$ form, he went and worked as a teacher, in part, to help educate his twin brother. However, he continued studying as a private candidate and passed A-levels and was admitted to the University of Nairobi (Kenyatta Campus) for his Bachelor's degree. Kenyatta

Campus later became a full-fledged university, Kenyatta University.

I believe that God works in mysterious ways and his works are manifested in us. Ogembo and I crossed paths once again when I was promoted to become a Staffing Officer in Kisii District. Before he joined the university, I hired him as an Untrained Teacher (UT). We later lost contact and I was happy to learn that he proceeded to the United States for further studies and became a professor. We occasionally talk over the phone.

> **Biographer's Note:** *In a cellular phone interview, Prof Justus Ogembo had the following to say from the United States:*
>
> *"Stephen taught me from grade 5-7. He mediated between me and my harsh environment. Without him, I do not know what God would have done with my life. Enough to say, he facilitated my going to Kisii High School. At Kisii, the late minister Joshua Angatia, retired Headmaster Motanya Moenga, Bob Hancock and Andrew Marfleet tried, each in their respective and uniquely personal ways, to help me navigate through poverty, but Providence dictated otherwise.*
>
> *"God designed that 'when the fullness of time came', the contributions of each of these men would be coalesced into a consistent whole to thrust me beyond my circumstances into what I am today.*
>
> *"I can also confirm to you that Sarah Angima was my classmate at Nyansiongo DEB Primary School. Her father, Anderson Angima was a pillar of faith in the early days of settlement of Abagusii in Borabu Settlement Scheme. He and a group of elders led prayers for us just before we sat for the Kenya Primary Examinations (KPE). We were the pioneers of the school. One of us joined Alliance High School, two Kisii School. Five proceeded to Cardinal Otunga High School-Mosocho, and one to Itierio High School, among others.*
>
> *"Stephen Mabea was a disciplinarian but with a tender loving care. He esteemed and idolized administrative structures. He did his best to shine in whatever rank he found himself. When you get in touch with him, tell him that I am fond of him and thankful to God that my life trajectory crossed with his."*

Another of Mzee Mabea's student, Francis Rosana said the following:

"I am happy that God saw it fit that I be one of Mwalimu Mabea's pupils at Nyansiongo Primary School. He was a very dedicated and organised teacher and administrator who ensured that he put everything in place for us to excel.

"Due to his efficiency, I cannot remember a day when learning was disrupted at the school. Wherever we were in school, we always felt his presence even when he was not physically with us, be it in class, playground or dormitory. Mwalimu was basically on duty day and night, all year round. Mwalimu was very strict but humorous. He would warn pupils promptly. The discipline he instilled in us has kept most of us upright. Personally, I have traversed the world in the line of duty and I always made reference to the lessons I drew from mwalimu.

"I have a very strong attachment to Mwalimu Mabea whom I saw as a role model. He is someone that people, especially those in the teaching profession should emulate. His devotion to duty stood apart and I believe if teachers do the same, their impact on humanity will be felt more.

"Mwalimu Mabea never stole the learners' time. In fact, he stole his time and gave it to us. Although his home was in Mecheo area that overlooks our school, he was on duty for the better of the week, day and night.

"The school is located in a rural area and on our own, we could hardly find someone who had excelled in education and emulate him. To fill the void, Mwalimu invited motivational speakers to the school. Through this, our view of life was broadened. We realized that we had to upscale our dedication to studies if we needed to excel in life.

"When we meet as old students, we go back to the fond memories of our teacher. I have his cell phone and once in a while, I give him a call. Then we happily jog down the memory lane. I know he is very proud of us and this is why I have maintained the connection."

- *Francis Rosana is a retired Accountant. After Nyansiongo, he got his O-level education in Maseno School, and then proceeded to Cardinal Otunga Mosocho for A-levels. Thereafter, he joined the University of Nairobi. He has worked in Kenya, Tanzania, Sudan, S. East Asia, among other places.*

Prof Richard Nyamwange had this to say:

*"Mwalimu Mabea taught us in Standard Six. He was a very good and devoted teacher. I remember my classmates including Peter Aching'a, Salome Kinanga, Charles Osinde, Justus Ogembo, Ratemo Kereni, and Francis Rosana. Mabea's son Zablon Agwata was also in the school. We all succeeded in our academics, partly due to Mwalimu Mabea's dedication to prepare us from the formative stages of study.*

*"He was a hardworking and focused manager. This is why he was moved to Kisii Primary School, and then promoted to be Assistant Education Officer. He went on to hold various administrative positions in Kisii and Siaya and left a legacy there.*

*"We as old boys and girls are coming together in a bid to give back to the school that made us. Our visit to the school will mark a wonderful reunion. Mwalimu Mabea continues to be the glue that binds his former pupils together, long after we left Nyansiongo.*

- *Prof Richard Nyamwange studied Economics and has spent most of his career life in the United States.*

The following brief account was given by Dr Shem Oyaro, a former pupil of Mzee Mabea at Nyansiongo DEB Primary School:

*"Mr. Stephen Mabea was my headmaster the whole of my primary school life. He taught us Science, a subject I did well during my final exam in 1972. A disciplinarian, he made tremendous contribution to our education. He is a man I hold in high esteem. He influenced my career path and I became the first one from Nyansiongo DEB Primary School to eventually study veterinary medicine.*

*"Nyansiongo used to be the heartbeat of sports. I remember a girl qualified for the Olympic Games but her parents declined to let her go due to scepticism associated then with foreign travel. Mr Mabea mentored us and I doubt if our academic record at the school will ever be broken."*

Another pupil, Dr Julius Ogeto who is a retired Consultant Physician and Sports Doctor based in Nakuru said the following:

*"The school was doing very well and that is why my elder brother Adson Ogeto transferred me from Nyakongo Primary School to*

*Nyansiongo. I stayed with Mwalimu Mabea's children including Zablon within the school compound. All teachers stayed within the compound and had their meals together, except breakfast. Mostly, we ate ugali and sukumawiki (kale).*

*"Teachers were very devoted in their work and Mwalimu Mabea was a go-getter and able captain. I remember that teachers could correct each other while having their lunch. They always challenged themselves to improve their mean standard scores.*

*"I cannot recall Mabea being absent from school even once. His towering presence kept teachers and learners alike on toes at all times. He could walk behind the tuition block, his hands held to the back, ostensibly to monitor if learning was taking place. He instilled high level discipline on teachers and pupils alike, and this has helped many of us in this life."*

Nemwel Atemba, an author in his own right, was Mabea's pupil at Nyansiongo DEB Primary School. Concerning his teacher, he had this to say:

*"I have never met a teacher who can match Mabea. He had a way with teaching to the extent that you could not forget his lessons. In fact, I can remember most of the things he taught me and how he framed them. He led by example and everyone in the Nyansiongo family had to walk in his footsteps.*

*"Mwalimu eliminated school absenteeism. He could visit homes of pupils who skipped school to find out why they did so. If they were trying to be mischievous, he prevailed upon their parents to give them rough time at home. When the young ones realized that they were under watch from home and school, they were left with no option other than attending school at all times. Some of Mabea's successful pupils today were not really serious with studies from the word go. They are enjoying the fruits that he made them grow."*

Consolata Mocha, a communications specialist, had the following to say:

*"I remember Mr. Stephen Mabea as a great teacher, disciplinarian and a man of foresight.*

*"I joined Nyansiongo DEB as a young girl and was at the school until 1970 when I sat for my CPE. On school days, I did a total of 15 kilometres daily, walking to school in the morning and*

doing the same after school to get back home. The distance was not a problem. I enjoyed the early morning walks and runs.

"As I moved to higher classes, I became more aware of my school environment. The Headmaster, Mr. Stephen Mabea, who was also my Class 7 English teacher, was very strict. You dared not fail because that earned you his unique pinch on your ears! It was a great 'wake up' call. You had to pass English! I however never earned his wrath much in this area because I used to do well in the subject.

"However, I remember that one time I was among several pupils who came to school late. We stood outside in the cold morning dew. To punish us, Mr. Mabea did not use a cane. Instead, his finger nails 'greeted' my ear lobes. By the time he was done, my body was on fire. Holding onto the ears, it didn't matter that I fell on the morning dewy grass. That was the last time I got late in the morning!

"Mr. Stephen Mabea was one of the reasons I and many, then young girls and boys, passed with flying colors to join national schools. He was a great teacher, a disciplinarian, and one focused on achieving results. He dealt with anything that threatened to stand on the way of his young pupils.

"He helped me and many others in Nyansiongo DEB to work hard, check our behaviour and proceed to Form 1 in good schools. Later, many of us proceeded to universities and later God blessed us with jobs.

"For my case, I joined Asumbi Girls' School and later Kipsigs Girls' High School for my Form V & VI. I then joined the University of Technology in Sydney Australia, School of Communication Studies, for my Bachelor of Arts in Communication. Later, I would undertake my Masters in Philosophy in Development Communication at the University of Ghana. I am currently doing my PhD in Communication Studies at Moi University.

"I worked with then Voice of Kenya (KBC), several NGOs and as World Bank Consultant for IFMIS Communication, stationed at The National Treasury, Nairobi Kenya.

"I am full of praise and thanks to Mr. Mabea and his teachers like Mr. Osinde the Maths teacher and others who invested in us and contributed to what we have become as adults in our beautiful country.

"Mr. Mabea, thank you for your commitment to a great course of raising young men and women of this nation who are now leaders in their own right."

Benedict Ongeri, a long time family friend of the Mabeas, now an economist and lecturer at the University of Nairobi said thus:

"Mwalimu Mabea never taught me in class. However, I learnt a lot from his lifestyle. This happened because his son Zablon was my friend. In fact, our friendship culminated in me being Zablon's best man at his wedding.

"Mabea had Volkswagen. Such cars were very few. In fact, his was the first one that I ever saw. I knew for sure that if I worked hard as he did, a day would come when I too would own a car.

# Destination: Kisii Primary School

If you get to Kisii Town today with your eyes closed, you will be enveloped by an orchestra of sounds. You will hear horns honking and motorbikes zooming past. You will also hear chattering people and footsteps hitting the paved walkways. If you open the eyes, your line of sight will be encompassed by a rising skyline and bustling and energetic people. The people will be walking in all directions, minding their business. You will also find sizeable vehicular traffic. Inside the bustling mingle you will not miss the surge of excitement and satisfaction of being in a vibrant town.

The status of the town today was beyond any imagination during the country's early days of independence. Locally, some people call the place Getembe (its traditional Kisii name) while others refer to it as Bosongo (the White man's' residence) or Boma. It acquired the name Bosongo because it was among the first settlements and administrative units of the colonial administrators. The name Boma may be an acronym, British Overseas Management Association[1]. The town is inhabited by people from many ethnic groups and races. Apart from Africans, Asians are very conspicuous. Some Indians have lived in the town from as early as 1920.

Located at the edge of the county's commercial and administrative capital is Kisii Primary School. The school is one of the oldest learning institutions in the town and its environs, having been established in 1957. It was initially the learning centre for Asian and European children, who were first admitted in March, 1957. It was initially called Hindu Primary School.

When my pupils in Nyansiongo DEB Primary School posted impressive grades in national examinations, the school topped the Gusii region performance chart. I received felicitations for leading a committed staff and placing the school at a proper

---

1   See Nemwel Atemba's *Abagusii Wisdom Revisited* (Nsemia Inc. 2010).

launch pad for success. At the time, the performance of Kisii Primary School was dismal despite the fact that it was a town school, better endowed with resources and admitted children from Asian families. It was also a preferred school for children whose parents were civil servants like the administrators. It was decided that I be transferred to the school to help improve its performance and ensure that it took its rightful place in the region's performance list. I left Nyansiongo in 1972, having handed over to Charles Maisiba.

When I reported to Kisii Primary School on May 1, 1972, I found it in a mess. The majority of the teachers were Indians. Some were Britons. I discovered that the teachers were using a syllabus that was strange to me. Prior to independence, African learners were subjected to the African Preliminary Examinations while the Asians and Europeans sat for a different examination. This was stopped after independence when the two syllabuses were unified. However, Kisii Primary School had not adapted the new syllabus.

It is not uncommon for human beings to be slow to adopt to change. When I took over the headship of the school from J. Jadeja, Mr Makwana continued to deputize me. I found that the teachers were ignorant of the new syllabus. They were also not quick to adopt and appreciate it. Instead, they were stuck to the old and outdated syllabus, oblivious of the fact that it was inconsequential in the study life of the pupils.

The more I took time to acclimatize myself to the new environment, the more I learnt that the challenge ahead of me was enormous. This was a giant school in terms of learners' population and teachers' numbers. It was double-streamed, unlike my former station which had a single stream. The size of the teaching staff was almost twice that of Nyansiongo.

The majority of the teachers at Kisii Primary School also appeared ready to give me hard time. They wore belly bottom long trousers and never bothered to shave their hair. They called their hairstyle 'boogie'. The hairstyle was popular in the country at the time. However, I was taught in college that a teacher should dress and carry himself or herself modestly. I was not going to bend this important professional requirement. I did not have many issues with the female teachers. Many of them were Asians and they dressed modestly in line with the Indian tradition.

My other worry, however, was chronic lateness of both teachers and the learners. Poor time keeping is the hallmark of indiscipline. I had to fix these issues first.

I knew that if I was going to succeed in my mission at the school, I had to start by instilling discipline. To curb lateness, I made a grill door that led to the staffroom and tuition block. The door was in clear view from my office. In the morning, I would be the first one to arrive, and then close it when the official working hour struck. This forced teachers and pupils who came late to be stranded at the gate. I then used the opportunity to warn them about coming late to school. I emphasized that it was an abomination to get to school late without any good reason or permission. I also told the teachers to stop embarrassing themselves since I could not punish them for lateness just as I could reprimand the pupils. The message sank and I was able to curb the problem of lateness.

On weekdays, I stayed within the school compound and went home on Friday. The houses were few but modest, compared to those at my former station. I was leading from the front in observing time and in the three years I worked at the school, I only got late once. This happened when my car had a tyre puncture at Kegati along the Keroka-Kisii road on one Monday morning. As was my routine at the start of the week, I was travelling from my rural home to school. I had purchased this car from my savings while at Nyansiongo. However, because I mostly stayed in the school, and only went during the weekend, I literally underutilized the Voxwagen. At Sh9,000, the car was a major investment for senior teachers and education officers.

Earlier, I had convened a staff meeting and directed the teachers to observe modesty in dressing. I also told them that, henceforth, it was wrong for any teacher to come to school with unkempt hair. I gave them instructions to pass through my office the following morning, for me to confirm that, indeed, they had heeded the directive. This really got them worked up. However, they did not have an option other than towing the line.

I had another hurdle. A majority of the teachers did not understand the basics of teaching as a professional job. For example, they could not make the master time table. Worse, even if I gave them one, they could not generate their class and personal time tables. This compelled me to request the District Education Office to post two qualified teachers to the school. The education office heeded the request and posted Haron Mweberi and Jean Champion. Champion was a Ugandan, married to another teacher (from her country). I jumped to the high heavens when I received the two trained and qualified teachers. I knew I stood a better chance of revitalizing the school with their help.

It is standard practice that a staff meeting is held once new teachers join a school. When we held ours, I learnt with dismay that the old staff members were reluctant to receive the new teachers. This happened largely because, unlike the incoming teachers, those who had been at the school were not professionally trained. They were not qualified to teach.

We shared teaching subjects and allocated each other responsibilities. One Sunday, I discovered that my deputy, Mr Makwana, was backbiting and undermining me quietly. When I made a forward move, he looked for ways of pulling me backwards by inciting teachers, to the effect that I was overworking them. However, I discovered that he was equally incompetent in handling responsibilities as my deputy, given what the role required. For instance, left to him, he could not effectively handle indiscipline cases, let alone whip teachers to do the right thing in my absence. I recall that, one time, I asked him to make the master time table, and he was unable to do it properly. I could not approve it because it did not reflect all subjects, teachers and number of lessons in every class per week.

I was disappointed but I did not want to embarrass him. Instead, I drew Haron Mweberi's attention and asked him if he could make the school's master timetable. "That is a very easy thing for me," Mweberi said.

"How many hours do you need?"

"Give me one hour."

True to his word, Mweberi mounted the school master timetable on the staffroom wall about an hour later. I was pleasantly impressed as the other staff members spoke in hushed tones.

"Ensure you have your class timetables ready in twenty minutes," I announced to the teachers after congratulating Mweberi. A wave of disquiet jolted the room. No one was about to talk. But I could tell that they had something to say and I prompted them to speak.

"Sir, I don't know how to make a class timetable," said Miss Mina Shah.

"You must be a very honest person," I responded.

"Yes, sir."

"Who else has the same problem?" I inquired, and all teachers, save for Mweberi and Jean, put up their hands.

This was another disappointment. It basically meant that the old teachers could not extract information from the master time table to make class time tables. Basically, they could not even know or tell how to start the assignment. Mweberi and Jean came in handy in guiding them make both class and personal timetables.

From the events of that day, the old teachers knew that they needed to pull up their socks. They learnt that, for them to be up to their calling, they needed to work closely with the new members of staff. From then on, they humbled themselves to learn on the job.

Jean and Mweberi went on to assist them to prepare schemes of work. The two also offered guidance on making lesson plans and other documents for teaching, evaluation and assessment. It was the start of structured teaching at the school!

# Dealing with Segregation

When Europeans and Asians settled in Kisii town, they needed a school where their children would get education. The settlers did not imagine a situation where their children would mix with Africans for anything, including education. So, instead of mixing the children regardless of race, schools were segregated. In Kisii town, Asians' children studied at Hindu Primary School which was established in 1957. It would later be renamed Kisii DEB Primary School.

When the school admitted the first batch of African pupils, irrespective of the social and economic standing of their parents during my administration, there was resistance. In class, I noticed that African, Asian and European pupils sat separately. I thought that this was perpetuation of segregation hat would negate the fruits of our country's independence. But how was I going to solve this emotive problem without hurting the innocent children's conscience? My instincts guided me that the Indian parents would not easily yield to the idea of mixing their kids with Africans in the class sitting arrangement.

I retreated to my residence that evening, deep in thought. That night, sleep eluded me. I needed to find a lasting solution to the issue of segregation at the school if we were to succeed in the long run. The roosters were 'raving mad' at their morning duty when an idea popped up in my mind. At first, I thought it was a dream. So, I jumped out of bed for fear that, if I stayed longer, it would evaporate from my head. I had had such an experience before where I could not piece together details of a dream I just had a few minutes back.

After overseeing the smooth take-off of the new day's lessons, I drove to Daraja Mbili market. The open-air market is the largest of its kind in Kisii town. At the market, I bought two varieties of maize cobs. Some cobs had grains with one colour while others had different colours. Back in school, I took the two different maize cobs and displayed them to each class, at intervals. While I did this, I enquired from the pupils which cob impressed them. They appeared to fall to my wish when they all agreed that the cobs with two or more colours were more attractive.

By the end of the exercise, I had hung a maize cob with different colours at every classroom door. This mission coincided with the Continuous Assessment Tests (CATs). When the teachers ranked the learners, it emerged that their performance disregarded their skin colour. I then instructed the teachers to use the list generated from the students' performance to shuffle the arrangement of pupils in class. By the end of the exercise, the African pupils were mixed with the Indians and Europeans.

"You now look very attractive, just like this maize cob with coloured grains," I told the pupils when I went to their classes. They were all in agreement. I believe kids are innocent and loving creatures. This world would be a better place if we held the same virtues as adults. The gaps we have along tribe, race, religion or wealth are propagated by adults.

The majority of the Indian parents were not amused when they learnt what had transpired in school. This I could tell at a glance when I saw them drive into the compound the following day. They were led by Dr Singh and another person who was a magistrate. Their body language told me that they were going to be hostile, but I triggered a conversation anyway.

"You look agitated, what has happened?" I enquired from the parents.

"We have come to know why you mixed our kids with Africans," the magistrate replied.

My conscience was clear. I had not done anything wrong. My desire was to satiate the thirst of knowledge for pupils, irrespective of their backgrounds or origins. At the time, the District Commissioner (DC) was the Chairman of the School Committee. I knew it was going to be a tall order for me to calm the parents. I therefore hoodwinked the parents to wait for me under a tree shade as we entered my office with the magistrate for consultation. The legal practitioner was their spokesman.

"Let me call the DC to come and address the parents," I told the magistrate as I ushered him to a seat in my office.

"Why do you want to call him," he asked.

"I want to tell him that you have started segregation here as it happens in South Africa," I responded.

"No! Let me talk to them," he said as he hurriedly walked out.

There was pandemonium as the parents scampered into their vehicles. The magistrate had warned them that I was calling the DC and they were going to be arrested for advancing racial discrimination.

There was a lull and instability for a couple of days that followed. Some Asian parents withdrew their children from the school. This made me fear that the school would collapse. Dr Singh even made plans to flee to his country of origin - India - with his children. More parents would have followed him in droves. However, another stop measure made them dismiss the idea.

Dr Singh's wife was a Girl-Guide trainer. I approached her and told her to be visiting my school. She could then help Jean establish a Girl-Guide Club at the school. When she jumped on the idea, I knew I had scored against her husband and fellow Asians. This was for the good of their children.

When Mrs Singh came to the school, I briskly walked by her side. We chatted and laughed as she toured the school. In the evening, she went home with her daughter. As I gathered later, the daughter happily told her father that she was doing well and enjoying being in the school. Slowly, unity crept in and substantially sealed the racial segregation that was being perpetuated by a section of parents.

As an administrator, I was not out of the woods yet. I realized that, amongst the Asians, there were differences based on religion. Some were Hindus while others were Ismaili and subscribed to the teaching of the Aga Khan. The latter worshiped at the point presently occupied by the Aga Khan Hospital in Kisii Town. Their Hindu counterparts converged at a building opposite the hospital for their worship. Africans were Christians but they too classified themselves along denominational lines. Some were Catholics while others subscribed to the Seventh Day Adventists (SDA) teachings, the main Christian denominations in Kisii even today.

I visited the parents at their places of worship and homes and encouraged them to support the school. In school, we could give each religion and denomination a chance to present its worship items like songs. This excited the pupils. They even prepared various songs to present during music festivals. The divisional festivals which brought together schools from Bonchari, Kitutu and Nyaribari were held at Manga in present-day Nyamira County.

Jean Champion trained the Kisii Primary School choirs. In the competitions, the school presented a centre piece in Ekegusii which was titled, *Obori bwa Baba Ekeande.* The song spoke of a bumper harvest that saw a community thrive and lead a healthy life. It also speaks about a locust invasion that devastated the harvest. (Coincidentally, I am writing this story at a time when the desert locust invasion has affected several counties in the country). The thrilling performance secured position one in the competition. Word went ahead of us and reached Kisii town. We were welcomed to the town by jubilant parents, including the Asians who said that we had done the school proud. As the song implied, our school was productive and in the right direction. The racial and religious gaps in the school had been sealed for good!

## Simeon Nyachae Takes Note

There are some who say that a school is as good as its head teacher. But to me, I believe that apart from visionary leadership, it takes teamwork, discipline, hard work, dedication, and combined sacrifice for a school to do well in academics and non-academic activities. Once we were over with the hiccups at the start of my tenure, I enjoyed massive support from parents and the government to steer Kisii Primary School forward. The government posted more African teachers while majority of the Asians quit voluntarily since they were untrained.

In 1973, my deputy Makwana left and returned to India. Haron Mweberi was promoted to deputize me. Mweberi was a very dedicated teacher. He later rose to serve as the Secretary of the Kenya National Union of Teachers (KNUT), Kisii branch. He has since passed on.

The school posted a steady rise in examination performance. In the 1973 national examinations, it took position three in Gusii. This was history in the making. Ululations rocked the air as parents jammed the school to witness the results. For the first time in the history of the school, several learners received admission letters to national schools. Several others were admitted to provincial and district schools. Most of them went on to excel in their secondary school education and were able to join universities and other tertiary institutions for further studies.

Simeon Nyachae is one of Kenya's senior statesmen with a long public service record. When I held the helm of Kisii Primary School, Nyachae was at his prime in terms of age and career. The school is about 8 km from his ancestral home in Nyosia. At the time, he served as the Provincial Commissioner of the former Central Province which was headquartered at Nyeri. The position of Provincial Commissioner has since been scrapped, thanks to the Constitution of Kenya 2010.

Following the shining grades posted by Kisii Primary School, Nyachae was impressed. All along, his children studied in schools near his workplace. However, he was concerned that, as a public servant, his sojourn was denying his children an opportunity to be home where they could learn Ekegusii and Kisii culture. This is one of the challenges that civil servants who valued their heritage faced. Whenever they got transferred, they had to move with their families. The best alternative for them was finding the children schools where they could experience minimal or no interruptions as a result of the transfers.

One morning, I received a call. On the other end was the District Commissioner for Kisii, David Mulama. By virtue of his position as the chairman of Kisii Primary School, we were always in constant touch. But this morning, he sounded quite excited. After a chit-chat, he told me that he had a visitor in his office.

"My senior Nyachae is impressed with the performance of your school," he said. "He is asking for permission to bring two of his children to the school."

I had not met Nyachae before. However, he was a reference point whenever I told my pupils to work hard in their studies. A chance had struck for me to come face to face with one of the Gusii community's great sons.

I went to the DC's office with two blank admission forms, to meet Nyachae. As soon as I entered the office and closed the door behind me, Nyachae rose from the chair. He was a brown, energetic man, wearing a broad smile. We shook hands while he congratulated me. "I have closely followed your work and I am impressed by what you have done at Kisii Primary. Keep it up," Nyachae said to me.

It did not take long before two of his children (Samuel Maragia and Noah Ndemo) reported to Kisii Primary School. Nyachae is a person who respects order and appreciates good work where it is done. His mien tells it all. He had been briefed by the DC that lateness was greatly loathed in the school. He said his children must toe the line. To ensure his sons made it to school on time, he availed a pickup and hired a driver. The driver would chauffeur the children to school promptly in the morning and take them home in the evening.

When the children sat for their examinations, they were among the others who excelled. Nyachae was very happy. He invited me for lunch at his Nyosia home. Although he was away, I was treated as a Very Important Person (VIP) by his wives. A goat had been slaughtered. In the house, a sumptuous meal awaited me. I could whiff the broth in the bowls and it did not take long before I was served. After eating, I was given some raw meat to take to my family. His wives also gave me several pineapples too to take home.

**Biographer's Note:** *Mwalimu Mabea served as the head teacher of Kisii DEB Primary School for two years (between May 1st 1972 and June 3th 1974). A visit to the school is quite telling of the kind of a man Mabea was. Although its present state speaks of neglect for a school in an urban centre, the headmaster's office tells a different story.*

*The office doubles as a mini boardroom. On the wall right behind the head teacher's chair, four photographs are hung, next to the school headship roll. Of the four images, three may be familiar to most Kenyans for they are full colour portraits of Presidents Daniel Moi, Mwai Kibaki and Uhuru Kenyatta. Sandwiched between Kibaki and Moi's is the imposing black/white image of Stephen Mabea during his prime at the school in 1974.*

*A typewritten footnote under the photo reads: "In his farewell party, it was proposed and accepted that his photo be kept in this office in memory of his good work during his Headmastership." The decision is attributed to the parents of the school at the time. The school has had twelve head teachers since its inception. Patel was the pioneer and served between 1957 and 1966 when he passed the baton to J. Jadeja. Jadeja, who was of Asian origin just as his predecessor, served up to May 1972 when he handed over to Stephen Mabea, who was the first African to head the school. It is quite historical. History is playing itself again at the school. Of the twelve head teachers who ever served at the school, eleven were male. Presently, Grace Nyamweya is the head teacher and has been at the helm since 2014. She is committed to lead her staff in delivering results so that she leaves a mark that would be told and retold as Mabea did.*

*Although Mabea left the school nearly fifty years ago, his name is chronicled to this day. During my visit to the school, I randomly sampled the views of teachers, some who could be the age of Mabea's grandchildren and interestingly, they all know about the retired teacher as one who left an indelible mark at the school. I also gathered that a number old pupils including some from Mabea's time who are now serving this country and the Diaspora in different capacities have formed an Alumni Association and have embarked on giving back to the school that moulded them at that early age.*

*At the same time, Jean Champion who was Mzee Mabea's staff mate said on the telephone from her home in Vihiga County that he was a dedicated, forthright and focused school headmaster.*

*"He was a wonderful team player. I never met a dedicated teacher like Mr Mabea during my sojourn in teaching," she said.*

I studied here and came back as a teacher

The first classrooms at Nyansiongo Primary. They are being used to date

Pupils of Nyansiongo DEB Primary School go for lunch on Oct. 15, 2020

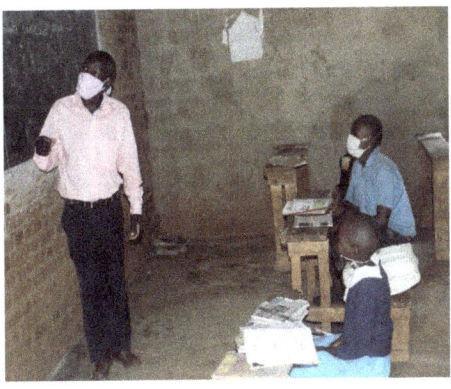

A teacher with Standard Four pupils in one of the oldest classrooms at Nyansiongo DEB Primary School

Boys play outside the first classes of Nyansiongo DEB Primary School

When the white settler left, we converted his servants' quarters to teachers' houses & pupils' dormitories

Other classrooms at Nyansiongo DEB Primary School. Some were built during the time of my headship

This secondary school is a product of Nyansiongo DEB P. School. The two are separated by a fence

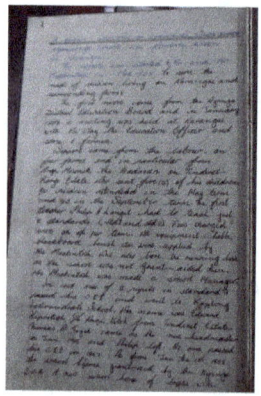

An extract from the Log Book for Nyansiongo DEB Primary School

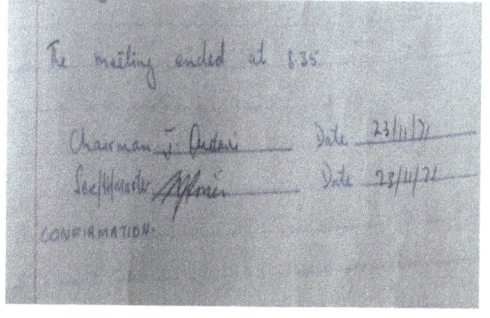

I signed these minutes of the school as was my tradition

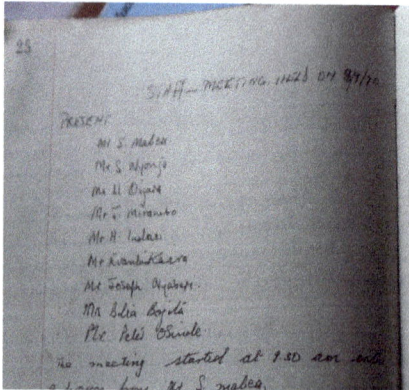

An extract from Nyansiongo DEB Minute Book of 1970

With staff mate Jeremiah Omasire at Kisii DED Primary School

My portrait taken and displayed at Kisii DEB Primary School

This roll shows that I was the first African to head Kisii DEB Primary School

A storey building at present-day Kisii DEB Primary School

I am seated at the middle accompanied by my Kisii Primary School staff

I attended a KNUT delegates meeting in Mombasa in 1970

# 3. ADMINISTRATION IN EDUCATION

# Another Turn

I did not stay at Kisii Primary School for long. It had increasingly appeared that I was becoming my seniors' 'Mr. Fix It'. After two years, the office promoted me to the rank of Assistant Education Officer (AEO) without being subjected to any formal interview. The promotion coincided with the mess at the Irianyi Divisional Education Office. Irianyi later became Kisii Central Division.

The mess at the divisional office was occasioned by external interference championed by some politicians. A section of residents aligned themselves to a particular politician danced to his tune as he intimidated education officers. This caused the interdiction of four divisional officers of the area in quick intervals.

At the time, one man called Bathromew Orang'i worked as the District Commissioner of the Northern Frontier District, now Garissa County. Orang'i is a common name in Kisii whence he hailed from. He was well-known because he was the first person from the Kisii region to join Makerere University, Uganda. So, to many people, he was known as the Makererian.

One day, Orang'i did the unimaginable. This was the time of the Shifta War, in which the Northern Frontier District (NFD) agitated to join the Greater Somalia. History has it on record that the British took over administration of the NFD with the promise that it would be returned once the two countries became independent. When Kenyatta and the British reneged on the promise following Kenya's independence, secessionists started a guerrilla war that came to be known as the Shifta War. It occurred between 1963 and 1967. The Shifta War is blamed for brutal killings and widespread violation of human rights in Northern Kenya during that time. This is according to a report published by Daily Nation on May 22, 2013 and attributed to the Truth, Justice and Reconciliation Commission (TJRC). "The report released by TJRC says officially, 2,000 people were killed during the Shifta War waged between 1964 and 1967. However, the report notes that unofficial estimates place the death toll at 7,000," said the newspaper report.

Orang'i was at Garissa at a time when the area was

experiencing insecurity, a spill over from the Shifta War. Confrontations between the police and criminal gangs often ended in bloodletting and deaths. Reportedly, when Orang'i learnt that elected leaders from the area were party to the insecurity, he made them to lie prostrate on the ground and thoroughly caned them. The incident hit the headlines for a number of days.

Such news had never been heard of before. Indeed, it turned out that the highest office in the land was equally perturbed by this rare act. Orang'i received a call from President Jomo Kenyatta. It was reported that the President told him that however wrong the Members of Parliament were, he should not have caned them. The DC was then moved to Kisii perhaps for security reasons, but I am not sure if he was really assigned specific roles at the new station. However, I could see him working closely with the then Kisii District Commissioner (DC) David Mulama and the District Education Officer (DEO).

While in Kisii, Orang'i could come to my office at Kisii Primary School. This way, he had a chance to learn how I ran the school. I later learnt that this was the man who travelled to Kisumu and told the Provincial Education Officer that he knew a teacher who could fix the problems that dogged the education office in Irianyi Division. I think that all along, the District Education Officer (DEO) and the District Commissioner (DC) did not know that they were being assisted to fix what was giving them administrative headache. I too did not know that someone was lobbying for me to be propelled to such a position.

The letter elevating me to Assistant Education Officer (AEO) was written by the Provincial Education Officer, through the District Education Officer (DEO), Kisii. It instructed me to take over as the AEO of Irianyi Division in a week's time. The letter was delivered to me by the DEO. When he realized that I was pleasantly shocked, he told me that I was born to grow, and never to remain static. Soon, I handed over the school to John Gichana who was a close ally of the late Dr Zachary Onyonka. At the time, Dr Onyonka was the MP for Kitutu Chache Constituency which has since been split into Kitutu Chache North and Kitutu Chache South constituencies.

## Sweeping Irianyi

The education office at Irianyi division was a jumbled mess. There was outright prejudice that negated the value of education. Locals flashed the clan card and regarded 'non-locals' as outsiders who should only be seen and not heard. A particular elected leader had alienated the non-locals, with intent to micro-manage schools within the division. This type of clan balkanization affects schools in various parts of this country to this day.

Because of this established mode of operation, any Assistant Education Officer who reported to the station was supposed to literally go on bended knees whenever the politician spoke. The AEO had to yield to the whims of the politician, otherwise he could not survive at the station. The fierce politician was surrounded by retrogressive advisors but he took their word as final on delicate matters like the education. This precipitated a steady decline of academic standards in the division since the AEO was presumed to be a toothless stooge. If he raised his voice, he paid a price for it.

Before I reported to the station, the District Education Officer warned me that the challenge ahead of me was enormous. According to him, Irianyi was a difficult station. It needed me to be tough and ready to make landmark decisions, he advised.

Once at my new station, the politician never came to me. Instead, he contacted me through proxies. This did not please me. However, this being his modus operandi, I knew I did not go to the station to change him forcefully. I remained firm but reasonable to his henchmen. Much as I listened to them, I never bowed to pressure or attempt to make any unprofessional decisions. Instead, I told them that I would not relax my work ethics and make decisions that contravened the state of my conscience and the teaching profession.

For instance, they expected me to be tough on teachers who

did not hail from the immediate community and be soft on the 'sons and daughters of the soil'. I strictly told them that teachers were professionals whose work surpassed clan limitations. I also advised parents to put the interests of their children in school at heart, ahead of clan and political inclinations.

Non-local teachers were highly mistreated and I needed to put a stop to the worrying trend. I recall one case that puts my assertion into perspective. At the time, there were concerns that the headmaster of Ibacho Primary School was mismanaging the institution. Apart from being the headmaster, he was the chairman of the local branch of the Kenya National Union of Teachers (KNUT).

He had caused the interdiction of one teacher who hailed from Bobasi Constituency on claims that the teacher was a habitual absentee. I was shocked when the teacher's interdiction was brought to my office. I was justified to be taken aback because; I had neither received, nor forwarded the headmaster's report to the District Education Office for action as established procedure dictated.

When I investigated the matter, I found that the date the teacher was present, he was marked absent. I further established that on the material day, the headmaster was absent. I also interrogated the teacher's schemes of work, lesson plans and pupils' notes to get watertight evidence.

I found that, according to the records, the teacher was in class on the material day. He taught, gave assignments and marked them. This was evidence that he had worked. Upon checking the same documents for the headmaster, I discovered that he was absent on the material day. The headmaster had therefore usurped his powers and made wrong allegations to plunge the teacher in hot soup.

I left the school with the evidence and proceeded to my office to compile a report. In the report, I exonerated the teacher and recommended that action be taken against the headmaster for misrepresenting facts to harm his staff member. This expropriation and malice was unacceptable. When the disciplinary team from the Teachers' Service Commission headquarters held a meeting in Kisii, it was shocked to find that my report and the headmaster's were conflicting.

The commission turned on the District Education Officer. They sought to know if the DEO cross-checked the headmaster's report with me before he made the decision to interdict the teacher. He denied, and admitted to the team that he relied on the headmaster's report which he assumed to be accurate. The commission sternly warned him never to leave a stone unturned before undertaking such a decision that carried landmark ramifications on a teacher.

For the first time, the TSC interdicted the headmaster cum KNUT Branch Chairman and reinstated the teacher he had victimized. This shook every corner and the centre of Kisii. The news also reached the KNUT Headquarters in Nairobi. Their eye in Kisii had been 'smashed'!

At the time, Joseph Kioni was the union's Secretary General. Kioni stepped in to rescue the branch chairman. Sobriety and wisdom prevailed when Kioni said that for the sake of unity and co-existence between the union and the teachers' employer, the headmaster should be warned, pardoned and reinstated.

The news reverberated across the land. Supporters of the embattled headmaster were shocked that he could have been interdicted. This taught them that, in the teaching profession, no one was indispensable. Education stakeholders in Irianyi Division also appreciated the fact that teachers were posted to local schools in the interest of their children and nothing else.

As I adapted to the station, I convened a one-week seminar for headmasters in the division. In the meetings conducted at the present-day Gusii Elders' Council office precincts, I told the school administrators not to misuse their positions but uphold integrity and serve diligently. With the help of the DEO, we cascaded the training to assistant teachers. In the training, we told them to observe time and other guidelines as enshrined in the TSC code of conduct. Gradually, the levels of teaching in Irianyi Division improved.

# My Inspection Duties

My first car was a Volkswagen Beetle. It was a small, oddly shaped, inexpensive and fuel-efficient family car. Very few people owned automobiles at the time and my type was one of the most beloved in the country. Its uncanny ability to capture imaginations of children and adults alike is still ingrained in my memory.

A car was also a status symbol and an indication that one was economically thriving. Most importantly, it came in handy to help me in my school inspection roles. I could get to a school at 8 am, ready for a full day's work, with packed lunch in the car. This enabled me to witness how the school utilized time, which is a key resource in life.

To ensure minimal, or zero disruptions of learning, I parked the vehicle some distance from the school and covered the remaining part of the journey on foot. Often times, I could find the teachers flat-footed. When I got to the school, I first marked those who attended the assembly. When pupils dispersed to their classrooms, I inspected how the teachers handled them there. At lunch hour, I disappeared to relax and have lunch in the car. I then returned to the school for the afternoon session.

After this rigorous and intensive inspection exercise, I retreated to my office to compile a report for the school. I then forwarded it to the Inspector of Schools (now called Quality Assurance Officers) for advice and action. This made the inspectors fix their eyes on my division. At the same time, it made teachers who were working in my area of jurisdiction to be more vigilant and work within the confines of the TSC guidelines. They knew that if a teacher got three warnings, he stood the risk of being interdicted.

Teachers handling pupils in lower primary had serious challenges. However much they wanted to give the learners a firm foundation, they lacked teaching materials for vernacular,

Ekegusii. This bothered me because Ekegusii was the main language of instruction in the early classes.

I identified one teacher who was good at drawing. His name was Ben Morwabe from Nyabara Ibere, West Mugirango Constituency. Morwabe and I drew and named domestic tools, containers, animals and weapons in Ekegusii. We also drew a few wild animals. Then, we compiled the drawings in a pamphlet. The pamphlet assisted teachers in the whole of Kisii to impart knowledge to the learners. It is rather unfortunate that my copies got destroyed in a fire that mysteriously burnt my house. However, I thank God that other items were rescued and no life was lost or injuries suffered. I hope that someday, I will lay hands on a copy of the pamphlet. Someone somewhere could still be having it in his or her library.

# Staffing Duties

On June 26th, 1976, blood pounded in my ears while the heart thudded in the chest. My feet tingled. My vision disfigured. My fingers shook violently. I had just arrived at my office and sat down. This had been my work station for slightly over two years. On the table was a letter enclosed in an envelope. It was from the Ministry of Education, clearly labelled 'Confidential' and addressed to me.

Well, it was not my first time to receive a letter enveloped in such a manner. But I was not expecting a letter at that time. When you are an officer, you receive various correspondences. You too do several others. What could be the contents of the correspondence this time? Why was I that anxious?

I reached for the letter. As I opened it, I felt like the tip of my nose had wetted. I took a deep breath, and then threw myself backwards to lean my head back on the chair. However, upon unwrapping the letter, I realized that there was nothing to worry about. I had received a promotion and should be happy!

The letter, signed by the Assistant Education Officer (AEO) R.K. Towett appointed me to be the Staffing Officer (SO) in charge of Kisii District. This was a great honour. It indicated that my career progression was on the right trajectory.

When education stakeholders in Irianyi Division got wind of the letter's contents, they were saddened. They murmured in protest and vowed not to let me go, but their murmurs did not tempt my appointing authority to rescind its decision. However much the Irianyi people wanted me to stay, I wanted to leave. Leaving the station to take up bigger responsibilities was the surest way that I intended to progress career wise.

Up to this stage, I was still a P1 Teacher certificate holder. I took up my new office in Kisii district headquarters with zeal and zest. That September 3rd, 1976 I was promoted to Secondary (S1) Teacher on merit. The promotion did not come on a silver platter. I had evidently worked for it at my former station and the record spoke for itself.

At my new office, I was in charge of all teachers in Kisii District. Specifically, I handled their recruitment, promotions and transfers. As well, I sat on the disciplinary panel and was the custodian of all teachers' files in the district. Quite a number of things happened at the time, some of which compelled me to make landmark decisions. Such decisions affected some individuals who masqueraded as teachers and threw them off the teaching profession. When they fell to the wayside, their positions were rightly given to qualified teachers.

A case in point occurred in 1978. I had gone home for leave when I was summoned to resume duty before expiry of my leave period. When I reported to the office, I learnt that the government was aware of the fact that it did not know the exact number of teachers in schools. The government was concerned that, on the ground, some schools were understaffed. The number of teachers on the payroll was higher than it was in the schools.

All along, teachers had temporary identification numbers. To unearth and fix the anomaly, the government sanctioned a headcount of all teachers in the republic. As the Staffing Officer, I was directed to forget my leave and undertake the coding and registering of teachers within my area of jurisdiction.

This was not going to be a walk in the park. According to records availed to me, the district was overstaffed. But on the ground, pupils in some schools got insufficient attention due to inadequate number of teachers. The headcount exercise was going to get rid of ghost teachers and save taxpayer's money. But on the other hand, I did not know the fate of whoever made it to the list of shame once we concluded the exercise. My predecessors in the staffing office had never unearthed the scandal. Was I going to break the ice?

I thought soberly, deep and hard. Then I came up with a formula. I prepared declaration forms, which would be signed by headmasters of every single school in Kisii. In the form, they were required to file details of their teachers.

The details included the names of teachers, their grades and the year they joined the school. The headmasters were then required to append their signatures at the foot of the forms. By appending signatures, they were affirming and swearing that they had accurately captured the information to the best of their knowledge and verified it.

At the time, teachers' pay slips were received in bulk at the office of the District Education Officer. When the employer dispatched the payslips for January 1978, I retained them in the office. In the meantime, I waited for the headmasters to return the declaration forms to me.

When they were all done, I went through the completed forms alongside the payslips. In the scrutiny, I sorted the slips whose owners' names were captured in the declaration forms. I then affixed them to the forms and returned them to the headmasters. By the time I wound up the scrutiny, it dawned on me that over 350 payslips were unclaimed since they did not have corresponding names in the declaration forms.

I typed the names appearing in the unclaimed payslips in a circular then circulated it to all schools. According to the circular, any teacher who had not received his payslip was required to come to the office to claim it. Of the over 350 in the list, only six turned up. Apparently, the six had missed out in the listing by their headmasters for unclear reasons.

My major concern, however, was that we had over 350 teachers who were on the payroll, earning without working. I gave a copy of the ghost teachers to the Teachers' Service Commission (TSC) for further action. The affected 'teachers' may have gnashed their teeth, but in silence. I never received any complaint or accusation of unfairly dismissing anyone. They quietly retreated to their homes to find other ways of earning an income. As they did so, the commission mandated my office to hire the same number of teachers. The watertight recruitment drive narrowed the teacher shortage in Kisii to some extent.

My employer, the Teachers Service Commission (TSC) was excited by my steadfastness. As I noted earlier, the issue of ghost teachers was not confined to Kisii alone. Instead, it was replicated in various parts of the country. This challenged the teachers' employer. It meant that the commission was taming criminals unknowingly and depriving innocent children the opportunity to interact with able and qualified teachers.

In recognition of my efforts, the commission invited me to train other staffing officers from all over Kenya. The one week training took place at the Kenya Institute of Education (KIE) which has since been renamed the Kenya Institute of Curriculum Development (KICD). When my counterparts implemented my strategy, Kenya eliminated ghost teachers and sanitized the teaching profession. I may not have the exact number of those who were affected nationally, but in Kisii, 350 individuals lost income that they had been earning illegally.

This added a promotion in my bag and enhanced my profile. I was promoted from Job Group G to H in recognition of the exemplary work I had done. On top of the promotion which affected my salary upwards, I became the Acting District Education Officer.

# Ten Percent Recruitment

When I look at the mess in our education sector today, I wonder when and where the rain started beating us. I get worried because many public schools are understaffed. The few teachers in our schools break their backs in imparting knowledge and skills to the children. While at it, thousands upon thousands of trained teachers wallow in poverty and joblessness. This unreasonable scenario continues to compromise the efficiency and output of serving teachers.

The sector was on the right path 30-40 years ago. For example, the government prioritized the training of teachers. Trainees underwent rigorous training at college or university level. Upon completion of training and graduation, the teachers were recruited almost immediately. This made teaching one of the most preferred and cherished professions.

In 1979, I was at the centre of the placement of newly recruited teachers in Kisii District. As per government instructions, we were required to hire a number of teachers, equivalent to ten percent of the existing teaching force in the district. Each district across Kenya was required to do the same. This, the government envisioned, would further narrow the teacher to pupil ratio significantly.

Once again, I discovered an anomaly that was likely to throw the recruitment drive and posting into disarray. I noticed the recruitment directive disfavoured some communities. I guess if the incident happened today, it would have been a subject of intensive investigations. I guess so because many of those who received letters of appointment at the time and reported to my office for posting bore similar names and hailed from Central Kenya. Some men carried names which indicated that they were female and vice versa. I could not understand how this happened.

At the time, Mrs. Wanderi was the Provincial Staffing Officer in Nyanza Province. She was my boss at the provincial level. However, although she was in charge of Nyanza Province, she was stationed at the TSC headquarters in Nairobi. When I informed her of the anomalies that I had detected in the new recruits' letters, she expressed shock. After a lengthy discussion on the phone, she promised to get back to me after consulting the Principal Staffing Officer.

The phone conversation relieved my troubles. I thought the burden was off my shoulders. I was wrong! I discovered that I was not out of the woods yet when Mrs. Wandera called back and directed me to use my wisdom.

Whenever I got confronted with a scenario that would make me to take a tough decision, I became more circumspect and treaded carefully. First, I retreated to my house, freshened up, had a meal, and then stretched in my bed. I then retraced the start of the issue at hand, looked at possible solutions, and then weighed them. If I did not find an answer, I gave myself time to do so. I never wished to make decisions in haste, only for them to backfire. This problem solving strategy that I implemented after close consultation with my seniors and confidants in Nairobi worked for me once again.

I evaluated the bearers of the recruitment letters, one by one. In the evaluation, I asked them deep oral questions with a keen interest to know if they were capable of teaching. It dawned on me that despite the anomalies in their names as captured in the letters, they deserved an opportunity to teach as they were qualified. I then updated Mrs. Wandera and went ahead to post the teachers to schools within my area of jurisdiction, Kisii District. The office, just like the teachers, was grateful. Officers at the head office in Nairobi confessed to me that I had displayed unmatched wisdom and saved their face. They also vowed to reward me someday.

Time for my reward did not last an eternity. Instead, it came faster than none of us anticipated. In 1980, there was another teacher recruitment exercise, famously called Tripartite Teachers Recruitment. This was less than a year after the 10% exercise that culminated in the promise made to me by my seniors.

The government had once again directed that we recruit into the service untrained teachers. Anyone who had the Kenya Junior Secondary School Education (KJSE) certificate and was interested in the job would apply and get absorbed. I received several forms to distribute to Kenyans who were qualified and interested to teach. At the back of my mind, I knew that if the officers at the head office meant their word, this was the time they would help me. A time had come for me to test their commitment to the promise they had made to me the previous year. If they honoured the promise, many people from my community would also 'eat the national cake' by joining the teaching force in their numbers.

I covered the length and width of Kisii District, combing for potential teacher recruits. By the time I was done, over 3,000 young men and women who had a minimum of the Kenya Junior Secondary Education (KJSE) certificate had filled the forms. After ascertaining their accuracies, I carried them in a box to the Teachers' Service Commission (TSC) headquarters in Nairobi.

At the time, the TSC was housed within the city's Central Business District (CBD). The officers laughed when they saw me arrive with the carton. I told the officer who was handling the recruitment that I had come for their help and exuded confidence that I was certain that they would accord me the help I sought.

It was approaching 2 pm when I arrived. After handing the forms to them, they invited me for late lunch in the Milimani area. Over lunch, they assured me that they had a workable formula that would capture my interests. I remember that at the time, Milimani was a bushy area with a few business establishments. It never crossed my mind that the area would play home to the modern high rise buildings which you see there today.

I returned to Kisii a hopeful man. But even in the midst of hope, there was room for doubt. I was well aware that promises were never binding. They could be honoured or forfeited. If the later happened, I wondered what explanations I would give the job applicants.

Not long after, I was propelled to the top of the moon when the TSC absorbed all the 3,000 applicants into teaching. The newly-hired teachers were posted to various parts of the country, especially to Migori and Homa Bay. This generated a national debate, with a local newspaper carrying a story titled, "Deportation of teachers from Kisii." The story mentioned that Kisii had taken the lion's share of the employment slots. In the midst of the nationwide disquiet, the people of Gusii received the news in positive stride.

Some officers in the system were not amused when they learnt that I had a hand in the successful recruitment of the thousands of teachers from Gusii. To the detractors, my star as a man of the people was rising too fast. They thought time was ripe for them to trim my powers and dim my ambitions right in time.

The onerous task of 'trimming me to size' rested on one Mr. Charles Etale's shoulders. Mr. Etale, the District Education Officer in Kisii, appeared to have dropped from the blues to frustrate me. Although he was an education officer, he did not behave like one. Instead, he appeared to carry a vendetta against me. I could clearly tell that he was determined to strike hard and smash my career.

He started by transferring me from the district headquarters in Kisii to Nyamache Division. This was a silent demotion, given that I was in charge of the district before then. I promptly reported to my new station. Perhaps he expected me to resist, so that he could find an excuse of dirtying my file and thus put my job on the line.

Despite acceding to his directive, he did not leave me to settle down. Instead, he openly slandered my name. He unashamedly told education stakeholders in gatherings that I had over-employed teachers. It did not impress those hearing the message. Soon, they would teach him a lesson!

**Biographer's Note:** *True to Mabea's account, he played a critical role in recruiting hundreds of young people from the present-day Nyamira and Kisii counties into the teaching profession. During the period of interviews and writing this book (which lasted months), I came across many of the beneficiaries of this gesture.*

Interestingly, many of these teachers have since retired or are at the tail end of their careers in the profession. Richard Mecha is one of them and he is now enjoying his retirement. He had the following to say:

"When the government decided to hire hundreds of untrained teachers, I had just finished my secondary school education. Beneficiaries were required to fill forms and then get posted to schools outside their districts.

"At the time, Mzee Stephen Mabea was the Staffing Officer for Kisii District. He indiscriminately gave this opportunity to young men and women from all over Kisii District. In fact, I know more than a hundred teachers who entered the teaching profession through his assistance.

"Just as others, I was supposed to be posted outside my district (then Kisii) but when I made a request to him, he directed me to report to Sironga SDA Primary School.

"I will say that Mzee Mabea is a statesman and a role model that should be emulated. Our people in positions should help others without discrimination. This way, their names will stand out as the people who shaped their communities and country. The government should bestow honour upon Mzee Mabea in recognition of his illustrious career"

Roy Akumu who retired at the rank of Senior Inspector of Schools said thus:

"I come from a marginalized clan that lives at the Nyamira-Homa Bay border. Some people view us, the Abayengwe clan, as Luos while others say we are Abagusii. As a result, when it comes to the sharing of resources, we are often tossed between the administrations of Nyamira and Homa Bay.

"During the tripartite recruitment of teachers, I was a Zonal Inspector while Stephen Mabea was the Staffing Officer in charge of Kisii. The two of us worked closely and I identified over a hundred people from my area that had the prerequisite knowledge and qualifications to teach and they were hired by the government. These people transformed our area, for the better. At the time, I was among the handful of people who were salaried. Again, there were no kickbacks at the time and all the beneficiaries of the recruitment paid nothing in return. "I will describe Mabea as a focused, loving and dedicated Kenyan who left a mark in the education sector."

# 4. WHEN TROUBLE COMES

# Etale is Kicked Out

Recently, I saw a message circulating on social media platforms. It said something to the effect that, 'even if you allow people to step on your stomach, some will complain that you were not soft enough.' In this world, you will not be accepted and appreciated by everyone even if you dropped like manna from heaven, let alone your best in your work on earth. Indeed, that I was fished out of Kisii Primary School to assume expanded administrative responsibilities did not make everyone happy.

For me, 1981 appeared not to be my year. I had many problems to worry me and few reasons to smile about at my place of work. It appeared that Charles Etale, the District Education Officer, was determined to destroy my career completely, for reasons he knew best. I had the urge to protest loudly but I understood that his time of oppressing me would come to an end someday.

He had just come to Kisii and transferred me to Nyamache Division on flimsy grounds, with instructions that I would serve in the new station as the Assistant Education Officer (AEO). This came as a shocker to me since I was the Staffing Officer in charge of the entire Kisii District at the time. Therefore, although it was not expressly captured in the transfer letter, I had been demoted silently and accorded fewer responsibilities. This was sad but it did not worry me much since it did not affect my job group and salary. So, I moved to the new station to be in charge of Nyamache, Sameta, and Nyacheki zones.

However, in his bid to familiarise himself with the district, Etale arranged to hold meetings with education stakeholders at the divisions. In the meetings, he directed that Assistant Education Officers (AEOs) must accompany him. Although I felt that he did not like me, I had to obey his directives to avoid more trouble with him. Indeed, at his position, he had the powers to make punitive decisions including demoting me or causing me worse damage. For example, he could report to our employer that I was sabotaging him, an act that could put my job in the line.

As time went by, it became evident that he was either going personal against me or being mischievous. At one education event at the Manga Divisional Education Office, Etale stood me up for a dress down. He loudly and clearly told participants that I had messed education in Kisii. As he unashamedly branded me names, I felt like my blood was boiling in my veins. It was very clear that he had gone overboard. However, I restrained myself and ensured I did not lose my cool.

I doubt if Etale had done due diligence to understand how I related with the majority of stakeholders present at the meeting. Having streamlined the recruitment of teachers in the district, I had acquired substantial goodwill with many of them; I was not a pushover. For example, education stakeholders had complimented me for cascading the recruitment of teachers to the divisional headquarters, a move that ensured that available slots were evenly distributed across the district. We had conducted the hiring of teachers at Ogembo, Keumbu, Manga and Nyamira, among other divisional headquarters of the time. This move enabled me to confirm that the job seekers hailed from the respective divisions from where they applied.

So, when I read the listeners' faces, I realized that they were not happy with what they were hearing. There were spontaneous murmurs from the back of the hall. It appeared that the room was either too hot or had been invaded by some parasites which had disrupted the calm that was there before. Before Etale could figure out how to wind up his speech, the late Zachariah Angwenyi shot up and told him to shut up and leave the venue immediately. Zachariah Angwenyi was the chief for the area, a powerful national government administrative post at the time. Angwenyi also doubled as the Senior Chief in the entire Kisii District.

To the disgruntled participants, Etale had stepped on the wrong peddle. He hurriedly left following Chief Angwenyi's order.

Soon after the showdown that prompted Etale to leave the meeting, a majority of stakeholders sustained their concern that there was witch hunt against me. A section of Abagusii opinion leaders, including Chief Zachariah Angwenyi convened a meeting at the Kisii County Hall. Their main agenda was to establish why I was experiencing difficulties at Nyamache where I had been posted. They wanted to understand if Etale was being honest by claiming that I contravened any work-related code of conduct.

The deliberations from the meeting did not stop the fact that my seniors had made a decision to kick me out of Kisii District. On June 8th 1982, I received a letter transferring me from Nyamache to Siaya District. I would continue serving as the Assistant Education Officer (AEO) for a division that I would be allocated once I reported to Siaya District. (Presently, Siaya is one of the 47 counties in the Republic of Kenya.) My transfer appeared intended to punish me. Normally, I should have been transferred locally. Apart from that, I had not served for a reasonably long period of time at Nyamache Division to necessitate a transfer.

As directed, I headed for Siaya District.

Shock awaited me at Siaya. I got to the District Education Office and was told that a zone had been created, called Ulanga. This was a far-flung remote part of the district, close to Lake Victoria. My mind tells me, to this date, that Etale was behind this transfer. Regardless of whether he had a hand in it or not, the friction I had with him was a factor. If he meant well, perhaps he would have recommended that I get a cross-district transfer on promotion. Interestingly, Etale was soon transferred to Eastern Province at the very time.

James Oyugi was the District Education Officer in Siaya. As they learnt of my new posting, some officials in the Ministry of Education wondered aloud. They could not understand why a senior officer at the level of Assistant Education Officer would be posted to a zone. James was instructed to move me from Ulanga. That was how I found myself in Boro Division of Siaya as the (AEO).

When you accept a government job in Kenya, you commit to work in any part of the country. So, even when you do not like your new station, you are confronted with the option of accepting that you have nothing to do other than work. Boro Division encompassed schools in Siaya Town and its environs. It was relatively urban compared to Ulanga.

Over time, I adjusted to the reality at hand. It was possible that I was going to spend a substantial number of years in Siaya. Since birds of a feather flock together, I mapped out people from my Kisii community who worked or stayed in Siaya. After establishing the network, we agreed to formalize our presence in Siaya as a group. At the start, we were about fifty members. We therefore formed Abagusii Welfare Group, which brought together people who hailed from the larger Kisii. One of the members of the group was Michael Mayaka, a carpenter who had a workshop in Siaya Town. He hailed from Bonchari Constituency, Kisii District. He was a very active member of the welfare group. As members, we could meet monthly and catch up on developments and inquire into each other's wellbeing. Our overall aim was ensuring that none of us suffered in silence in the distant land.

> **Biographer's note:** *I established that the welfare group was Stephen Mabea's brainchild. Patrick Nyangenya, who is still a member, confirmed in a telephone interview that the group is still active. However, according to Nyangenya, it was renamed Nyamokia Group. Nyangenya further revealed that members credit Mzee Stephen Mabea for initiating the welfare group's formation.*

I will be departing from the truth if I say that the manner in which I was transferred from Kisii to Siaya never affected me. Ordinarily, it had to. No human being would wish to be transferred from his station of work on flimsy grounds as it happened to me. Indeed, as I observed earlier, I was literally being punished for working hard and ensuring that I upheld fairness and transparency in the office. Some people resist transfers and rush to the employer to beg that they are reinstated or given an alternative softer landing. However, for me, it was clear in my mind that when I got employed, I agreed to work in any part of the country. To me, I believe that when you get transferred be it in good heart or malice, you have the opportunity to work even harder at your new station. This way, you prove your detractors wrong. Such challenges at the work place may be meant to break you. However, you have to take them in positive stride. When you shine, those who expected you to stray eat humble pie.

I applied the very script I used in Kisii to get Boro Division out of the woods in the academic frontier. I could visit schools for inspection and encourage teachers to pull up their socks. Those who were lax were now on toes. The trickle-down effect was good results posted by learners in their examinations. At the time, good news spread fast despite lack of technological transformations that would come much later. It did not take long before word of my good deeds reached the desk of Peter Oloo Aringo who then served as the Member of Parliament for Alego-Usonga constituency.

# My Encounter with Peter Oloo Aringo, MP

When Peter Oloo Aringo spoke in the 1980s and early 1990s, friends and foes alike knew that Alego-Usonga constituency was ably represented at the national stage. Aringo was first elected to Parliament in 1974. He was allied to Jaramogi Oginga Odinga, then a bitter opponent of President Jomo Kenyatta. This is the fact that left Aringo confined to the backbenches in parliament. When Daniel arap Moi assumed power in 1978, Aringo's fortunes also changed. He kept doing a sea saw between two extremes: sumptuous service as Minister of Education and later Local Government, and powerlessness for example when he was dropped from the cabinet.

When I was posted to Siaya, Aringo was one of the most vocal legislators in the Kenyan parliament. At the height of his loyalty to President Moi, he was elevated to serve as the Minister of Education. He is famously known to have uttered, during a graduation ceremony at the University of Nairobi, that Moi was the 'prince of peace'. This remark attracted mixed reactions, with some of his critics saying that he had failed to draw the line between loyalty and sycophancy.

On the ground, Aringo was very close to the electorate. He had mastered the constituency like the palm of his hand. On weekends and when the House was on recess, the MP could spend much of his time traversing the vast Alego-Usonga constituency, inspecting projects, launching new ones or catching up with his constituents.

Over time, a section of politicians in Kenya have received their fair share of criticism for attempting to negatively interfere with education matters. In some cases, elected leaders attempted to micro-manage institutions. In other cases, they tried to manipulate officers for their whimsical aims. When the officers failed to dance to the politicians' tune, the wayward politicians would push for transfers of the officers or mobilize residents to stage demonstrations in an attempt to eject or have them transferred.

For Aringo, the situation was different. Education was very close to his heart, for he believed that it could turn around the lives of his people and Kenyans in general. Since he had his ears to the ground, it did not take long for him to learn that schools in Bori Division were gradually performing well in examinations. The remarkable performance of the division impressed him and, using his networks, he was able to establish that I had given my all to his people. Consequently, he sought me out; we met and struck a rapport that would rapidly rise faster than I ever thought.

The politician learnt that I operated under a tight schedule, daily. I spent most of my time in the field, inspecting schools, establishing their challenges and recommending to teachers what they could do to improve their overall performance. Since I did not have a car, mobility was often a challenge.

A keen education stakeholder, Aringo could request me to share my diary with him. I did not have any problem doing this since it was in the interest of the people that the two of us were serving. Aringo could amaze the constituents when he occasionally picked me from the field and took me to his house for a chat over a meal before he dropped me in my place of residence, a stone throw away from his. He could also visit me in my rented house in the evenings or pay me a visit in the office.

At the time, President Moi typically dropped bombshells and made ground shaking appointments, dismissals and other high impact pronouncements via the state broadcaster, the Voice of Kenya (VoK), present-day Kenya Broadcasting Cooperation (KBC). Senior personnel in government, especially ministers, dreaded listening to one o'clock news! This mode of operation made the president increasingly unpredictable. Those who served in his Cabinet never sat pretty for they knew that they could be reshuffled or dropped without advance notice, something that they usually learnt through a radio news item. Members of Parliament who were in good books with the President would also get pleasant surprises the same way and be elevated to the Cabinet.

One afternoon, Aringo picked me from my office and we headed to Siaya Town. While engrossed in a conversation in his pick-up, oscillating around academic standards in my area of jurisdiction, an announcement was made on the radio.

"*Mtukufu Raisi Daniel Arap Moi amefanya mabadiliko katika baraza lake la mawaziri* (His Excellency President Daniel arap Moi has shuffled his cabinet,") the news anchor opened the story.

Suddenly, Aringo who was in the middle of saying something jerked, then increased the volume on his radio. His face dazzled when it was announced that he had been appointed to serve as the Minister for Education. It was a warm surprise; a shocker!

To celebrate the news, he stopped the car. We stepped out and had a jig by the roadside, attracting curious bystanders. Being in his constituency, the onlookers were familiar with his car and they quickly joined us in the dance. To them, their leader had been given additional roles and powers to serve the nation.

On my part, I looked up to greater support now that he had become a minister in a portfolio directly linked with my job. Aringo was not alone in cheering me for my commitment to my job. The local branch of the Kenya National Union of Teachers (KNUT) was equally upbeat. The union leadership was in agreement that, although I was hard on teachers, I upheld honesty, and professionalism and my actions were devoid of malice. The unionists were updated to the fact that I could not witch-hunt or victimize their members, nor could I take a bribe to accord anyone a favour and disadvantage others.

*****

Following outright commitment by all stakeholders in the department education in the district, Boro Division topped in Siaya District in the 1984 national examinations. When the news hit the ground, there were massive celebrations. Parents as well as learners, thronged the Divisional Headquarters, all set to congratulate me. It appeared that, although success in examinations is not one man's job, they had taken note that I had offered leadership that was the basis for the good results.

Soon, a meeting was held at the Siaya District Headquarters. Among the invited guests was G. P. Oluoch who was the Director of Education from the Ministry of Education Headquarters in Nairobi. Although I was not quite conversant with the local dialect, I could tell that people were talking about me in hushed tones. They were also stealing glances at me. Others openly congratulated me as soon as our eyes came into contact.

Before the meeting kicked off, the senior officer from the Ministry of Education hinted to me that I had done an exemplary job in steering the division to performing well in examinations.

A bigger surprise that accompanied the compliment came forth when the officer rose to speak.

"Mr Mabea, kindly stand up and step forward," the officer said and I obliged, amid applause. "I have good news for you. You have been promoted on merit," the officer announced, arousing the meeting to clap, cheer and ululate.

At the time, a verbal statement from your senior at the rank of director was as good as a written document. Right in the meeting, it was made clear that I had been elevated to serve as the District Education Officer for Siaya District. This news was exciting and equally unsettling, for it meant that I would have an expanded mandate covering the entire district. It also meant that I would stay in Siaya for a while to come.

The news of my exploits in Siaya reverberated in the land and its effect was felt in my motherland, Kisii. Back home, people who knew how I was unceremoniously hounded out of my work station in Kisii and literally kicked out, were not amused that I was being useful to another community in place of helping our own. Their state of annoyance was fuelled by the fact that performance of schools in Kisii had steadily declined in a record two years. To them, they thought I should be rerouted to Kisii to execute the business that I left midway, that of making sure that we laid a solid foundation for the learners' future.

As indicated before, my transfer from Kisii to Siaya had appeared to be in bad faith and ill-intentioned, according to my own assessment. However, I had now put it behind me; it was water under the bridge. I was now focused on serving the Kenyan child, from wherever I would be working. After all, despite the geographical and ethnographical distances and boundaries, Kenya is one indivisible nation. I was being paid by the Kenyan tax payer and I had to work to justify the pay.

*****

In April 1984, a management training vacancy arose. I was directed via a letter to report to Siriba Training Teachers' College. The training brought together education managers and administrators from Nyanza Province. I reported to the college, ready to absorb as much knowledge as I could. The training brought together Assistant Education Officers (AEOs) and Assistant Primary Schools Inspectors (APSIs).

To my warm surprise, it turned out that the trainers during the in-service course had taken note of my abilities. Therefore, instead of dwelling on what they had prepared in their training module, they turned to me as a reference point to share with fellow trainees what had made a difference in Boro Division compared to other divisions. I was very happy to share my experiences with my fellow officers. I felt validated! Everything that transpired during the training is solidly ingrained in my memory.

*****

Around that time, a full-blown scandal involving the recruitment of teachers hit Siaya District. Since majority of the key administrative officers including the District Education Officer (DEO) were locals, it appeared that they retreated to their tribal cocoon to irregularly hire the teachers. Instead of according the available slots to qualified candidates, they dangled them for a few shillings. In the process, the opportunities went to the highest bidders to the chagrin of those who were better qualified. I was still working as Assistant Education Officer (AEO) and was one of the non-local people holding an administrative position in education office in the district.

Perhaps this exercise should have tainted my file, a thing that I dreaded most. However, it never did. I could clearly tell that my colleagues had sidelined those they perceived to be non-locals in the recruitment process. These outsiders were not many. One of them was from the Rift Valley. I too was considered a foreigner.

As a matter of procedure, all AEOs were supposed to be in the recruitment panel. This was not the case. Although we had worked harmoniously before, it was evident that they wanted the two of us to be as far away as possible from the recruitment drive for reasons that they knew better than we did.

Ordinarily, we should have joined them at the recruitment venue. Instead, on the material day, they left us in Siaya town, without disclosing to us where they were going. In the evening, we learnt that they had recruited several teachers behind our back and, as it turned out later, the process was marred with irregularities. This sparked discontent and outrage whose ramifications reached the State, prompting a probe by the Criminal Investigations Department (CID), now the Directorate of Criminal Investigations (DCI).

In their investigations, the CIDs who had treated money posed as desperate job seekers who were willing to part with any amount, so long as they got recruited. This caught the unsuspecting and unscrupulous officers who included the District Education Officer (DEO), Assistant Education Officers (AEOs) and Assistant Primary Schools Inspectors (APSIs) pants down. Not only were they nabbed but also interdicted.

The officers' letters of interdiction were delivered by Amina Shah, who was an Under Secretary in the Ministry of Education. Before a helicopter carrying the officer touched down, we had noticed the presence of heavily armed and hawk-eyed detectives hovering around Siaya County Council Hall where an education meeting was underway. The interdicted officers were served with their letters in the meeting and ordered to sign a delivery book to confirm that they had received them. It was a humbling experience for them. It was equally embarrassing. Above all, the move carried heavy lessons for attendees of the meeting.

The meeting had a surprise for me. All along, I did not know that the Under Secretary was carrying with him a letter confirming that I had been promoted to the rank of District Education Officer. When he handed it to me, I was exceedingly happy. Among other tasks, I was directed to appoint new APSIs and AEOs for the four divisions which formed Siaya District. These officers would fill the places of those who had been shown the door for flouting teacher recruitment guidelines in a bid to satisfy their appetite for quick money.

Aringo was openly happy when he learnt that my employer had recognized my work. He wanted me to stay in the district for eternity but this was not going to be possible for soon, I would be headed back to Kisii District.

President Moi was working overdrive to better the school environment and enhance uptake of basic education in the country. I was transferred from Siaya back to Kisii at a time when his administration launched the School Equipment Scheme and the School Milk Programme. As luck would have it, I was to be in charge of the two programmes in Kisii District. Overall, the two programmes had a huge impact in the sector. Kenya experienced an upsurge of learners' population due to the free milk that was provided by the government on weekly basis. The learners' health also improved tremendously due to the nutritional value attached to consuming milk. At the same time, pupils who could not excel in academic work were able to acquire skills in masonry, carpentry, and many other trades.

**Biographer's Note:** *President Moi died at a time of writing this biography. Kenyans who were in primary schools when his* *government supplied free milk recalled the time with nostalgia. They mourned Moi particularly for the milk, saying it was very sweet and always made them crave for more. As a result, they attended school without fail. Moi's free school milk model later collapsed but it has been replicated by Governors in a number of counties, notably by Hassan Joho of Mombasa.*

# 5 MAZIWA YA NYAYO

# The School Milk Programme

In 1985, a delegation from Kisii District made a journey to the Ministry of Education Headquarters in Nairobi, with my case in mind. This was instigated by David Onyancha who was serving as the MP of West Mugirango Constituency. We related well at a personal level and this was especially so because I had supported his election. Onyancha was accompanied by Mr. Stephen Michoma, a nominated Member of Parliament, and Stephen Mobegi the chairman of Kisii County Council. Unlike today when nominated members of the National and County assemblies do not have much say, Michoma was a very influential person at the time. The delegation wanted to petition the ministry to transfer me from Siaya to Kisii.

As I have already noted, the government had introduced the School Milk Programme and the School Equipment Scheme. According to the delegation, I was the right person to oversee the rollout of the two programmes in Kisii.

I later learnt that the ministry did not wish to release me from Siaya District. However, due to the pressure that the delegation mounted, the ministry yielded. At Boro, I had made several friends. However, many people in the locality could neither understand my operations, nor fathom how my leadership caused positive change. But the beauty of life is that people will want to be associated with performers. It was evident that schools under my care were doing well during my time at the helm in the division. This warmed the hearts of many local leaders and we easily bonded.

For instance, Paramount Chief Amoth Awira, the father of Siaya's pioneer governor Colonel Rasanga Amoth, warmed up to me. Gradually, the late Jaramogi Oginga Odinga, a doyen of opposition politics in Kenya, became my friend too. These two leaders were highly esteemed in Siaya. Many people in the area could wonder how, despite the fact that I did not trace my roots to the area, I related well with the two beyond the confines of my official engagements. Chief

Amoth and Jaramogi could invite me to join them under a tree for conversations that centred on what could be done to improve livelihoods in the area.

I have not come across an administrator and a politician relating so well the way Amoth and Odinga did. The bond between them was undeniably strong. They often told me that they were united for a purpose of development for their people and I was playing an active role in enabling them achieve it. Due to the closeness of the two, their wives equally made a concrete bond amongst themselves.

Before I got posted to Boro and became friends with Jaramogi, it never crossed my mind that our paths would ever cross a second time. Odinga had assisted me when I made an unsuccessful attempt to travel abroad in search of greener pastures. He had financed my trip back home from Mombasa where I was stranded.

> **Biographer's note:** *At some stage, Mzee Mabea thought of going overseas to pursue further studies. However, this dream never materialized. The story is captured in Chapter Two of this book.*

When news reached Chief Amoth and Jaramogi that I had been transferred from Boro, they had mixed feelings. Although they understood that as a government officer I could be transferred at any time and to any place, they thought that the transfer was ill-timed. To them, I should have stayed longer, to make their area the beacon of academic excellence that the rest of Kenya could envy.

With the local leadership accepting my employer's decision to move me to Kisii as irreversible, a historical farewell party was organized in my honour. The event was held in the precincts of my office and was attended by teachers, officers, learners, and administrators, among other education stakeholders. Speaker after speaker wished me well in my new assignment and asked me to go with them in spirit. I felt blessed. I have kept in touch with a number of people from the area and I understand many of the things that have transpired there since I left.

Before I left Boro, Chief Amoth presented me with a big he-goat and I can remember its appearance to this day. At the time, I had my car with me and it did not prove cumbersome to go with it home. However, on my way, traffic police officers flagged me down at Maseno. This appeared abnormal routine check, because they hardly searched private cars at the time. However, when they saw the goat in the boot of the car, they inquired from me if I had an animal movement permit.

"No, sir, I don't have a permit," I told them.

"Do you know that it is illegal to transport animals in this manner without a permit?" one of the officers asked.

"Yes, but this is a gift. I will slaughter it as soon as I get home."

"We will let you go but what you are doing is illegal," he said.

*****

I reported to Kisii District a happy man in January 1985. At the time, the government had started a new curriculum of education, dubbed 8-4-4. On top of this, it had launched the free milk school programme. These two programmes started almost simultaneously and were envisioned to complement each other. On the one hand, the milk would improve the children's health and raise school attendance. On the other hand, the new system was aimed at imparting practical skills alongside the theoretical facts the learners encountered in class.

When government funded projects start, they often experience teething problems. Some either stall midway and become white elephants or take ages to complete. This happens due to less than clear policies, hazy plans, sabotage and workers' resistance to change. The introduction of the 8-4-4 curriculum of education was not devoid of challenges from the formative stages.

When I reported to Kisii as the District Education Officer, I found the station in a mess. The prevailing conditions were precipitated by unclear guidelines on the purchase and distribution of teaching and learning equipment under the Kenya Schools Equipment Scheme (KSES) programme. I discovered that the docket was being handled by personnel who did not have a background in teaching. The officers lacked the knowhow in identifying the correct books and equipment fit for schools in line with the syllabus. As a result, the government was spending millions of shillings on books and equipment that would have little or no impact on the learners.

To change the situation, there was need to engage professionals. My concerns seemed to have been answered when the Ministry of Education issued a circular directing that Education Officers be in charge of the purchase and distribution of equipment to schools. These items would be used to teach and impart skills in subjects like Arts and Crafts, Home Science, Carpentry and Woodwork. The circular had bestowed additional responsibilities to my office and I had to deliver.

Even so, there was resistance and systematic underhand actions, by some, to sabotage the process. Ideally, the procurement of equipment was supposed to be done independently by my office. This was to lock out procurement officers who had no background in teaching. As I learnt, the plans to sabotage us were engineered at the Ministry of Education Headquarters. Apparently, a section of officers had formed a cartel with networks in the districts to benefit from public resources assigned to the programme. Through these wayward strategies, they could siphon resources meant for the equipment by exaggerating prices and/or quantities and qualities of the purchased items. At the district level, the resistance was raw and its ugly head needed to be smashed.

In government, handing and taking over is part and parcel of order when transfer of personnel occurs. Now that the tasks of KSES were squarely in the hands of education officers, formal handing over was necessary. Although the outgoing procurement officers had messed the KSES Programme, it was imperative that they handed over to the Education Officers. Part of the handing over entailed briefing the incoming officers on the tendering process for the equipment.

Well aware that the Education Officers lacked procurement skills, the outgoing officers took advantage to offer misleading information. This deliberate move was made so that the Education Officers would stand to fail. This scenario would then compel the ministry to revert the responsibility to the initial handlers.

Just like a majority of Education Officers, I literally found myself in turbulent waters since procurement was a new discipline to me. I resolved that this was yet another situation that needed God's intervention. Therefore, I ceded ground to my God to show me how I could navigate through the prevailing slippery situation.

I approached the Assistant Equipment Officers at the office. These were clerks in charge of equipment as well as the free school milk. In our interactions, I asked the officers to guide me through the tendering process. However, while at it, I discovered that they were deliberately misleading me. I had to find an alternative source of this skill that I desperately needed.

I remembered that I could get this precious information from books. Using a few shillings, I bought myself basic tendering and procurement manuals. In due course, the government issued head teachers with guidelines on how they could order the equipment for their schools, with further instructions that they do it in consultation with Education Officers.

With these guidebooks in place, I could see myself making a breakthrough in smashing the resistant cartels and streamlining the all-important government project, at least for my area of jurisdiction. I warned teachers to uphold honesty when making orders and emphasized that flouting the guidelines would be penalized. In due course, I was able to tell that the syndicate was not easy to crash since it had enjoined a number of head teachers too.

Over holidays, I quietly enrolled for a Procurement Assistant Grade Two course in Nairobi. At the end of the training, I was issued with a certificate of completion. When I got back to my station and engaged the Assistant Equipment Officers and head teachers, they discovered that I was more informed than they were on matters of procurement. I was now ahead of them!

Having understood the processes and prepared relevant documents, I advertised for tenders for the supply of equipment to schools in Kisii. When the advertisements appeared in the print media, the assistant equipment officers were appalled. Nevertheless, the exercise went on smoothly and each school was supplied with what it ordered for.

Late 1985, Mr. Alex Mutali who was the District Education Officer was approached by disgruntled officers on the matter of school equipment. The unsettled officers pleaded with him to move me from the district. However, the DEO turned down the request, to the chagrin of my rivals. Of all districts in Kenya, it was evident that Kisii had gotten the KSES concept right. There was a need for other districts to replicate our success if the project was to succeed countrywide.

When the Kenya Institute of Education (KIE) (now known as KICD) convened training for District Education Officers (DEOs) and Education Officers (EOs), Kisii was the centre of focus. In the training, the organizers asked my immediate boss Peter Mbugua (DEO, Kisii) to share our experiences and shed light on how we had managed to make a breakthrough in procuring and supplying equipment to schools in a process devoid of mischief and any trace of corruption.

"The exercise was executed under the leadership of Mr. Stephen Mabea who is the Education Officer for Kisii. I know he will be at a better position to take us through the process and I therefore seek your permission that he takes the stage," Mr. Mbugua said.

During the four day training, I literally became a consultant for the attendees. Officers could ask questions during my presentations or on the sidelines of the workshop. When the curtains fell, there was consensus that I had done a good job and should be rewarded with a promotion. As a result, I moved one job group to settle at K. This was not a mean achievement, considering the level I had started from.

In most jobs, promotions tag along with additional responsibilities. My letter of promotion was signed by Mr. Joshua Nyaboga who was the Deputy Director of Education. The letter indicated that henceforth, I would be in charge of the Kenya Certificate of Primary Education (KCPE) and the Kenya Certificate of Secondary Education (KCSE) examinations in Kisii.

By the time I retired, in July 1994, I was serving as Education Officer Two, in Kisii. Cumulatively, I served my country as a teacher and education administrator for about 38 years. In the entire period, I never received any reprimand, be it formal or informal from my seniors. This is with the exception of the tribulations I went through in the hands of a few people like Mr. Etale who unsuccessfully attempted to trip me. My file at the Ministry of Education was very clean.

As a result, Joshua Nyaboga who served as Deputy Director of Education and I were identified to be accorded the Recognition of Eminence (RE) in 1994. This was not a mean achievement. In fact, I had never heard or come across any other education officer who ever received this presidential recognition. The certificate was to be issued to me at the Attorney General's chambers in Nairobi. However, there was confusion, with concern that this was supposed to be a presidential award. I am still waiting for it.

Back in Kisii, a historical party was held in honour of my selfless service in the Ministry of Education. During the event, Mr. Peter Mbugua who had been promoted to the rank of Senior Education Officer and I were given several presents. These included a parcel of land each given to us by the Kisii County Council within Kisii Town. I later sold my plot to raise fees for my son's schooling.

**Biographer's Note:** *Peter Mbugua who was Mzee Mabea's immediate boss had this to say:*

*"I worked closely with Mabea for a couple of years. He was very instrumental in streamlining procurement of stationery and equipment for the larger Kisii District (now comprising of Nyamira and Kisii counties). Through his resolve to do things right, we advertised supply tenders and strictly vetted the applicants.*

This way, we ensured that we edged out briefcase suppliers who had previously swindled the government.

"Once the supplies were delivered to Kisii, we ensured they were dispatched to respective schools. At the time, I had a dedicated driver by the name Ogwoka who knew every corner of Kisii. I could visit the schools after deliveries and confirm that all was well. Once the headmaster confirmed receiving the items, we filled ledger books and filed delivery receipts for future auditing. The head of the school and I had to countersign the delivery documents too.

"In brief, I will describe Mabea as a very honest, hardworking, sincere and calm person. He is one Kenyan who appreciates that we were created by one God and we are one despite our ethnic backgrounds. This is why he never discriminated against anyone when we served the people of Kisii.

"Mabea's attributes may perhaps be hinged on his faith. I knew him as a dedicated Christian who practiced his faith. He respected authority and constantly consulted to ensure that he never flopped in his duties. Above all, he was very punctual and loved his job in totality.

"He was one of those officers you would turn to at any point. Through this good working relationship, schools posted impressive results in national examinations. For instance, when I left in 1989, two students from Kisii were among the top ten in the Kenya Certificate of Primary Education (KCPE). In fact, one of them topped nationwide while the other took position seven. The story was covered in the newspapers and I have retained copies to this date in my library. I was transferred on promotion as the Provincial Education Officer in charge of Rift Valley, a position I held until I retired."

# What Did I Go Home With?

In this life, getting a job is one thing and keeping it is another. I am proud because I served my country diligently as a teacher and education administrator until I retired. In all those years and in the stations I served, I never received any sanctions or threats of interdiction. Apart from the accolades I was showered with when I retired, I went home with my head high. Despite my humble beginning, I had touched and influenced several lives, straight from the classroom, sports and administration.

I noted earlier that after sitting for the Kenya African Preliminary Examination in 1956, I qualified to join Government African School (GAS) - now Kisii School. I joined the school with a vision and burning desire to study to the utmost I could. However, at the school, the administration diverted me to Kabianga for a teacher training course. This earned me a job at my former school Motagara in 1959. Ordinarily, I should have worked as a teacher until I retired. It was never the case.

This is what ignited my passion for studies. On 3$^{rd}$ August 1960, the Kenyan colony and protectorate issued me with the Teachers' Certificate. With the certificate in my bag, I taught for some years before I registered quietly and studied as a private candidate for the University of Cambridge Examination. This was a syndicated examination offered by the University in collaboration with the East African Examinations Council (EAEC). In 1970, I sat for the university examination and passed in all the six subjects that I enrolled: English Language, Bible Knowledge, Geography, Kiswahili, Commerce and Home Science. I was glad when I received the certificate that was signed by William Wetaiba for the EAEC and Owen Chadwick for the University of Cambridge.

I also studied and in 1973 qualified for the award of the Certificate of Education that was offered by the EAEC in collaboration with the University of Cambridge. This was two years after I was awarded a General Certificate of Education

Examinations (GCE) – equivalent to A-levels - in Religious Studies and Swahili from the University of London. These two certificates earned me a promotion to P1 Teacher. This was not a mean achievement at the time.

On May 2$^{nd}$, 1989, the Ministry of Education promoted me to Education Officer Two. This pushed me to Job Group J. I was over the moon when I received the letter of promotion, signed by D. M. Mutangili on behalf of the Permanent Secretary of the Ministry of Education. A few years later as indicated above, I received a letter of another promotion to S1, this time signed by G. P. Oluoch who was the Director of Education. This was the highest level I ever got in terms of formal education and promotions.

I have kept all my certificates, letters of promotion and other important correspondences with me. They form part of my greatest treasures. This is why, when my house caught fire some years back, I first reached for the documents in the cupboard before I rescued anything else. I wonder what I would be showing now as evidence that I went to school had the fire reduced the documents into ashes.

*Stephen Mabea*

Candidate's Registration No. W.1046/1956.

**COLONY AND PROTECTORATE OF KENYA**

**EDUCATION DEPARTMENT**

**KENYA AFRICAN PRELIMINARY EXAMINATION**

This is to certify that Stephen Aseri

of Motagara School

has passed the Kenya African Preliminary Examination held in the year 1956

having satisfied the examiners in the subjects noted below:

| | | | | |
|---|---|---|---|---|
| English | Pass | | Arts and Crafts | Pass |
| Mathematics | Credit | | Domestic Science Sewing | |
| Swahili or Vernacular | Pass | | Child Welfare and Nursing | |
| Geography, History and Civics | Pass | | Cookery | |
| Rural Science | Pass | | Laundry and Housewifery | |

Date 8/11/56

for Director of Education.

This certificate was issued without any alteration whatsoever.

G.P.K. 1012—10,000—4/56

**UNIVERSITY OF CAMBRIDGE**
**LOCAL EXAMINATIONS SYNDICATE**

in collaboration with the

**EAST AFRICAN EXAMINATIONS COUNCIL**

This is to certify that the candidate named below sat for the Examination for the East African Advanced Certificate of Education and qualified for the award of an

# EAST AFRICAN ADVANCED CERTIFICATE OF EDUCATION

The candidate passed at the level shown (Principal or Subsidiary) in the subject(s) named and attained the standard of the G.C.E. Advanced or Ordinary Level pass as indicated.

STEPHEN ARIERI MABEA                                                K901  518

|  | E.A.A.C.E. Standard | G.C.E. Standard |
|---|---|---|
| DIVINITY | SUBSIDIARY | ORDINARY |

SUBJECTS RECORDED ONE

EXAMINATION OF NOVEMBER/DECEMBER 1972

Chairman
East African Examinations Council         (See overleaf)

Vice-Chancellor
University of Cambridge

MINISTRY OF EDUCATION
JOGOO HOUSE "A"
HARAMBEE AVENUE
P.O. BOX 30040
NAIROBI.

2nd May, 1989

Ref. No. 11233/157

Mr./~~Mrs./Miss~~ S.A. MABEA

Thro'
District Education Officer
P.O. Box 79
KISII

FORWARDING

P/No. 11233/123

Date 31-5-89

A₃ D.E.O.

Dear Sir/Madam,

## APPOINTMENT

I am pleased to convey the decision of the Public Service Commission of Kenya that you be appointed to the grade of Education Officer II (Job Group 'J') with effect from 31st March, 1989.

The salary scale attached to this grade is K£ 2334 x 90 - 2604 x 108 - 3144 x 132 - 3408 per annum. You will enter the new scale at salary point K£ 2820 p.a. and your future incremental date will be 1st July.

May I take this opportunity to congratulate you for this well deserved promotion and wish you good luck in the future.

Yours faithfully,

D.M. MUTANGILI
for: PERMANENT SECRETARY.

**REPUBLIC OF KENYA**
**MINISTRY OF BASIC EDUCATION**

# Teacher's Certificate of Promotion

*Awarded to*

STEPHEN M. ARIERI

TSC No. 28610

holder of Teacher's Certificate Number P1/70/X.370

on promotion to the Status of S1 with effect from 1st January, 1977

Date 8th July, 1982    Signed G. P. Oluoch

*Director of Basic Education*

Certificate Number 994

# UNIVERSITY OF LONDON

003402

# GENERAL CERTIFICATE OF EDUCATION EXAMINATION
## JUNE 1971

This is to certify that

STEPHEN ARIERI MABEA
AT NAKURU, KENYA

passed in the following TWO subject(s):

ORDINARY LEVEL
RELIGIOUS KNOWLEDGE

ADVANCED LEVEL
SWAHILI                              GRADE B

Signed on behalf of the University of London      A.R. Stephenson

Secretary to the University Entrance
and School Examinations Council

Centre No.   Cand. No.
81070        01945

# 6. COMMUNITY SERVICE

# Politics, Trade and General Administration

Alongside my exciting, challenging and rewarding career in teaching and education administration, I had a relatively robust social and community life. From as early as 1959, I knew that no community would thrive economically, socially and spiritually if each person worked in isolation. This is why I made a deliberate decision to not only work with others, but also actively offer leadership when the need arose.

In 1959, while teaching at Motagara Intermediate School, I was elected to the position of Treasurer for Kerina Farmers' Cooperative Society. At the time, coffee was a major cash crop and foreign exchange earner for the country. Like my father and a majority of our neighbours, I had several coffee trees and earned modest returns at the end of the month. Of importance, Gusii coffee was said to be of high quality internationally, with its aroma rising to the high heavens and quenching the thirst of the consumers in various parts of the world. It also fetched relatively handsome returns. This is why small scale farmers affiliated to Kerina believed that the position of treasurer needed a forthright, open-minded and learned person who could account for every coin that belonged to the members.

The society drew members from Embonga, Kenyenya and Mokomoni areas. Then, many people in these localities had not obtained formal education. When they scrutinized the list of candidates who vied for the position of treasurer, a majority were in agreement that I was the most qualified. The verdict was confirmed in the society elections that I won with over 80% of the votes that were cast.

I was elected at a time I was an ambitious young man and I served the farmers with dedication. While in the society leadership, we were able to purchase a property in Kisii Town and named it Kerina House. The investment survives to this day under the same name. It is located opposite the Aga Khan Hospital in the fast growing commercial capital of Western Kenya. Every year, I receive dividends from the society because I have maintained my membership to date. However, is sad to note that fortunes of coffee farming dwindled over the years and very few people in Gusii still engage in coffee farming.

Separately, I represented Masaba Pyrethrum Farmers Union at the Regional Pyrethrum Board of Kenya in Nakuru. This was in order because in the Nyanza region, only Kisii District (now Kisii and Nyamira counties) grew pyrethrum. The crop did very well in Nyaribari, Bobasi, Kitutu East and North Mugirango regions. Unfortunately, as I have discussed elsewhere in this book, the pyrethrum sector collapsed years later just like the coffee sector. This dimmed fortunes from pyrethrum plunged many farmers into abject poverty. Some families have never recovered from the mess they found themselves in after the failure of the coffee and pyrethrum sectors.

*****

I have never vied or shown interest in any political seat, save for the time I thought of representing North Mugirango at the Legislative Assembly in Kisumu. Legislative assemblies were part of the 1963 Majimbo (independence) constitution but were later scrapped in 1964 when Kenyan adopted a republican constitution. I abandoned the thoughts of Legislative Assembly candidature soon after because Benson Kegoro, who had expressed interest in the same seat was my staff colleague at Motagara Primary School. Above all, Kegoro who went on to clinch the position, and later served as the MP for West Mugirango Constituency, is my cousin.

However, I should state that all along, especially during the hay days of my life, I paid a keen interest to local and national politics. I did this in the understanding that politics influences the lives of individuals and communities. In Kenya, politics is local and cannot be delinked from other aspects of life. However, unlike in the past, today's politics is shrouded in massive conflicts, hate, war-mongering and shameless and runway corruption.

At the national level, our founding fathers envisioned a country devoid of poverty, ethnicity, ignorance and disease. With the end of colonialism, Kenyans were optimistic that they would make gigantic strides towards the elimination of these drawbacks that had characterized their lives for many decades. But a closer look at our politics shows that the players engage while hiding dangerous cards under the table. This has negated our match to becoming a great nation. It has also precipitated a situation where the gap between the rich and the poor is widening by the day. It is a sad situation for it paints an image of a country where some people are 'more Kenyan than others'.

Politics has a tendency of swallowing up ideas that were formed with other motives. For instance, when we formed Keboye Welfare Club, it did not cross my mind that the outfit would later be used to dim political careers of some people and light others' political fortunes. The club was formed to bring members of Abagichora clan together so that they could venture into joint investments and fundraising for their children to join tertiary colleges and universities locally and abroad when such a need and opportunity arose.

In the early days of Kenya's independence, the entire Kisii District had seven locations, namely, South Mugirango, Kitutu, North Mugirango, Wanjare/Bonchari, Bobasi, Machoge and Nyaribari. The locations' boundaries acted as constituency boundaries too. At the time, the present day Wanjare and South Mugirango were one constituency; West Mugirango constituency was also part of North Mugirango. One of the installations that tell this story clearly is the North Mugirango Social Hall at Nyamaiya, in the present-day West Mugirango constituency. The historical building is one of the oldest in the region.

The people of West Mugirango wanted their area to be hived from North Mugirango, but they did not have an organized platform through which they could advance the idea. Through the activities of Keboye Welfare Club and other interventions, the government got convinced that North Mugirango had the numbers and deserved to be split into two constituencies. This also coincided with the change in the independence-era constitution that scrapped regional assemblies and the Senate, leaving a unicameral parliament. The newly created North Mugirango Constituency included Borabu Settlement Scheme and was referred to as North Mugirango/Borabu Constituency.

The influence of Keboye was, in part, responsible for weakening the influence of Siamani (Abanyamatuta) in West Mugirango. This was established by placing boundaries in such a manner that clans related to Siamani/Bonyamatuta, were hived off into North Mugirango. These are Abanyarorande, Abagesumi, Abagesinsi, Abombo, and Abakimori (the last three are also referred to as Abamwagamo). This may not have been my wish but the matter had overgrown me.

During the Andrew Ligale led Electoral and Boundaries Review Commission, Borabu was hived off from North Mugirango to become a constituency of its own. Presently, the people of Siamani who were earlier in North Mugirango form part of Borabu constituency. They form a formidable electoral block and the current MP Ben Momanyi has enjoyed their overwhelming support since the inception of the constituency. He is serving his second term.

Even with the new boundaries, the extreme ends of these constituencies speak a mockery of the territorial reviews. For instance, North Mugirango stretches from Sondu Township, covers the multinational tea estates bordering the Rift Valley and terminates at Chepilat. Borabu constituency on the other hand starts from Kiabiraa which overlooks Nyamira Town and adds onto the former Borabu Division. Were it not for other considerations like clan, the boundaries should have been created differently. Ideally, the review of boundaries should give attention to proximity of the people to the headquarters when in search of services. Therefore, Borabu should have comprised sections of North Mugirango, Kitutu Masaba and Nyaribari to generate sufficient population for the constituency.

For a long time, politicians from some parts of West Mugirango used the Keboye card to win elections. In its good days, the matrix worked for Joseph Osero Nyaberi and later David Onyancha. Onyancha first ran for parliament in 1969 and lost to George Justus Morara. He later represented the constituency in parliament for two terms, 1983-1988 and 1988-1992.

That said, the same Keboye card worked against them at some stage and they were humiliated at the ballot. Indeed, when Henry Obwocha entered the political ring, he successfully managed to weaken Keboye. This occurred because he had relatives in Bogichora where his mother Peninah Obwocha hailed from. The relatives threw their weight behind him as did Abasamaro. Obwocha went on to lead the constituency for three uninterrupted terms of fifteen years. This made the popularity of the Keboye outfit to evaporate as members disintegrated. Keboye is now a shadow of its former self!

# Establishment of schools

In the past, Borabu settlement scheme and other parts of Nyamira County appeared to be two different worlds. This was in terms of population density and the kind of agricultural activities residents engaged in. As discussed elsewhere in this book, Borabu was part of the former White Highlands where colonialist farmers owned huge tracts of land and practised large scale dairy and crop farming. When the white settlers exited, they sold their land and other immovable assets to people from various parts of Kisii who carried on with the economic activities, albeit on a fairly smaller scale. This was unlike in the other parts of Kisii where residents sub-divided land in line with inheritance practices and practised subsistence farming.

The situation has changed drastically in Borabu as well. There is massive sub-division of land both for inheritance and disposal purposes. Some of the present-day occupants engage in dairy farming. They also own fairly large pieces of land compared to their counterparts from the rest of Gusii (Kisii). It should also be noted that the scheme is cosmopolitan in nature. This is so because it is inhabited by people who trace their roots to various parts of the larger Gusii, and they are not organized along clan lines as it is in other parts of Gusii. The settlement scheme has in the past been seen as a place of the elites from the community. This may not be the case any more because some families in the area now lead a hand to mouth kind of life.

Sub-division of land is largely a cultural thing. However, it appears that the practice has hit the extreme. Space available for food production is diminishing by the day as the people put up more boundaries and buildings. For example, if a father owns an acre of land and decides to subdivide it among his four sons, this is what will happen: the land will have four natural or wall fences. Each of the sons will build at least a house and a pit latrine. He will also need space for his poultry or cattle. In such a scenario, there will be no space left for cultivation. If one owned an acre of tea and sub-divided it among his four sons, what will happen? Possibly, the yield will reduce because the sons may not have equal capabilities to manage the crop. The same applies to any other kind of farming. This is why Gusii region is staring at food scarcity and possible malnutrition. By any standards, this is sad news for the region that was once considered one of the food baskets in the country.

Leaders, especially in politics, have not confronted this matter, perhaps for fear of possible backlash. However, I think that the time is ripe for the people to take the bull by the horns. It is important for us to admit that this culture of sub-dividing land, a finite resource, is untenable. It is a practice whose time has elapsed. Indeed, in some places there are no open spaces for recreational activities. Most villages also lack space for communal gatherings like funerals. This is why you will find such meetings taking place in school compounds[1] or by the roadside, posing risks to the attendees.

However, I have observed that a few people have seen the logic in saying bye to land sub-division. In some families, members agree to pool resources and build storey houses, leaving spare the remaining space for other activities like cultivation. It is a fact that the costs of putting a storey building are prohibitive but the sacrifice is worth it, given that the space upwards is limitless. Some have demarcated space for buildings and the rest for food production. I think this is the way we should go as a community.

*****

When I was posted to Nyansiongo Primary School in 1963, there were a handful of families in Borabu. These families

---

1 **Editor's Note:** *these sentiments were developed before the outbreak of the COVID-19 pandemic. There are all indications that the pandemic would have an irreversible impact on how funerals are conducted. Accordingly to health guidelines, large gatherings are discouraged as a means of slowing down the spread of the disease. It is possible that people will get used with small funeral gatherings when the pandemic will be over.*

occupied expansive tracts of land and engaged in large scale farming. Due to the demand for labour in their farms, they employed skilled and unskilled workers and offered them accommodation. This enticed the workers to bring in their dependants (wives and children). In the prevailing situation, there was a need for amenities like schools, hospitals and churches.

In Borabu Settlement Scheme, I played an active role in establishing schools. As discussed elsewhere in this book, my first station was the present day Nyansiongo DEB Primary School. Previously called Narangai Primary School, it was established by Mackintosh, a white settler, in one of the farm houses. It was intended to benefit children of workers on his farm.

Despite the existence of the school, education was not a big agenda for the workers. Consequently, there were a handful of learners at the school. To rejuvenate the school, I needed to address the issue of low enrolment first, by approaching parents in the nearby farms and villages.

With the assistance of stakeholders like Chief Marario, we witnessed an influx of new learners to the school and ensured we retained them. Since Chief Marario hailed from Nyaribari Masaba, he managed to pull tens of pupils from there. I remember quite a number of my pioneer pupils at the school. They include Alexina Machanda, a girl who rose to become an outstanding athlete. In her exploits in sports, she conquered several races locally and abroad.

> **Biographer's Note:** *This is what Alexina Machanda said when I interviewed her for the purposes of this book:*
>
> *"Back in the day, athletics or sports in general were not quite rewarding. However, I enjoyed exploiting my talent. In school competitions, I participated in major towns like Kisumu and Nairobi. I also managed to participate in the 88 yards competitions in countries like Jamaica for the Commonwealth Games. That was the time when athletics legend Nyantika Maiyoro was a household name in the country. Mwalimu Mabea was very instrumental in training and encouraging us to exploit our potential on the track"*

As I noted earlier, Nyansiongo DEB Primary was the only existing school in Borabu when I first set foot there in 1963. Over time, we established that the number of families in Raitigo area was growing. This prompted us to establish Raitigo Primary School while Nyansiongo DEB quenched the thirst of learners from Chebing'ombe, Manga, Matunwa, Endemu and Mecheo areas.

*****

At Nyansiongo, with the influx of new learners every term, the numbers were proving to be more than the school could accommodate. We also sympathized with beginners (those in Standard One and Two), who, due to their age, were straining to navigate from their homes through bushes to be in school on time for lessons. There were also fears that they could be scared of animals like leopards that occassionally roamed in the thick bushes and shrubs. To ameliorate this challenge, I agreed with one of my teachers Andrew Ongaga to start Manga Primary School.

Manga Primary School started, in 1969 from a disused house that belonged to a white man who had since left the country. Vibrant, focused and determined, Mwalimu Andrew Ongaga happily accepted to be the pioneer teacher of the school, handling Standards One and Two learners. He did not have much at the start, save for a few pieces of chalk and blackboards that I gave him from Nyansiongo DEB Primary School.

In the early years of independence, navigating around Kisii was a herculean task. The road network was extremely poor and spotting a car in some places was a rarity. Due to this, it took sacrifice for education officers to go round inspecting schools on a regular basis. This is why it was understandable that Stanley Mayieka, who was the Manager of District Education Board (DEB) schools in Kisii, rarely visited the institutions.

One day, at around 10 am, I spotted a Volkswagen car at the entrance of my school. Such cars were not many and I did not need to consult my mind for long to guess that it was

Mayieka's. A friendly officer, Mayieka was a man of very few words when on duty.

While taking him round the school and giving him a briefing, he said to me, "I have not seen Mr Andrew Ongaga."

"Sir, Mr Ongaga is in charge of a school that we have started."

"Which school?"

"Manga Primary School," I responded.

Mayieka was evidently mesmerized with the news. The start of the new school had not been sanctioned by authorities and he was not sure if I was kidding him on such a heavy matter. He wanted to see and confirm what I was telling him.

With Mayieka at the wheel in his car, we got to the new school and found it in session. This got him excited as I heaved a sigh relief. What if we had found that Ongaga was not on duty? There and then, Mayieka admitted that the school sat in the right place and needed support to thrive. For a start, he elevated Ongaga to the position of Headmaster of the school. Just like that!

> **Biographer's Note:** *This is what Andrew Ongaga said about Mzee Mabea:*
>
> *"I briefly worked under Mwalimu Mabea at Nyansiongo DEB Primary School. He was a focused team leader. He is the one who identified me to be the pioneer headmaster of Manga Primary School. I think that were it not for him, perhaps, I would not have risen to the rank of headmaster or it would have taken longer. I kept consulting him on how to run the young school and he was always at hand to support me. We have kept in touch to date. Although I am now old and rarely leave my compound, Mabea occasionally visits me. We also speak on the phone regularly."*

*****

Before the government stamped its authority on the smooth running of schools, there were incidences where some churches were criticized for meddling in the affairs of learning institutions. This was so because the role of churches as sponsors of schools was not clearly defined. This created a situation where churches were overstepping their mandate. This happened because, apart from spiritually nourishing students, most churches did not invest any other resource in schools. Despite this, the churches had an upper say in the management of the affected learning institutions. This often precipitated a conflict, especially when academic standards got compromised. This was not the case some decades back.

While at Nyansiongo, I worked very closely with Rev Father Joseph Oucho who was in charge of the Catholic Parish in Uchuni. A devoted, visionary and no-nonsense person, Fr Oucho prioritized the establishment of new churches and schools. He was a firm believer in the philosophy that religion and education were inseparable. This endeared him to those in the community who had seen how the two changed lives.

When the need arose for a primary school at Chebing'ombe in 1966, we did not have funds at our disposal to start it. I approached Fr Oucho and shared with him this vision. As expected of him, Fr Oucho bought into the idea. He injected some resources from the church to kick-start the school. This was the actual and intended meaning of school sponsorship by churches! Parents whose children had suffered the long distance from Chebing'ombe, and its outlying areas to Nyansiongo DEB Primary School were very excited. They diverted their children to the new school. I am happy that it blossomed and continues to serve our people to this day.

The beauty of progress is that you never get tired of new ideas. With Chebing'ombe in place, we did not sit pretty and say that we had done enough. I knew that Mecheo area, where I had acquired land and settled, did not have a school, yet there were pupils walking all the way to Nyansiongo in pursuit of education. These pupils needed a school near them. That school had to be in Mecheo.

I approached my neighbours and gave them this idea. Although they supported it, some did not imagine that it could work since there was little money to support it. However, I told them that if we renovated a house that previously belonged to Peter Hill, who was the initial settler of the area, we could have the school there. Once this happened in 1966, the school attracted learners from Mecheo and Matunwa areas.

To sustain it, I approached Pastor Stanley Nyachieo who was the Secretary of all SDA-sponsored schools in Nyanchwa Conference and he promptly accepted to add it into his list.

However, there was a challenge. When Pastor Nyachieo was asked to give some money for the purchase of the Permanent Improvement Supply (PAI 337) and pay for the eventual issuance of the title deed, he was not at a position to avail the required amount. To fix this problem, he requested his cousin Paul Nyachieo, then a Clerk to Gusii County Council, to buy the land for the school. Paul was already known to me by the fact that his children were my pupils at Nyansiongo Primary School. He promptly paid for the PAI 337, affirming the start of the long journey that Mecheo SDA Primary School has travelled.

*****

Geographically, Nyansiongo is strategically placed in Borabu. This made it remain the central part of education activities. With primary schools in places like Raitigo, Mecheo, Manga and Chebing'ombe, there was a need for a secondary school in the area. We reasoned that establishing such a school would raise the number of learners who transited from primary to secondary school. In my mind, Nyansiongo was the most ideal for such a worthwhile project.

With this idea in mind, I approached the people of Raitigo and Manga in 1964. In our engagements, I asked them if they ever wondered of their children's future without secondary school education. In our deliberations, we agreed that it was prudent for us to start the secondary school close to Nyansiongo Primary School.

As I observed earlier, Nyansiongo Primary School sits on land that was owned by Mackintosh. On the land was Mackintosh's abandoned residence. So, the parents agreed that we start Nyansiongo Secondary School at the disused house. However, a local elite manoeuvred his way and took possession of the house before we could actualize our plans. This set us steps back to the drawing board.

The late Thomas Mong'are Masaki was a Member of Parliament at the time. Having worked with him as teachers at Motagara Intermediate School, I did not need to use proxies to talk to him. I laid bare the dream for the school, telling him that lack of land was standing on our way from achieving it. When Mong'are seized of the matter, it became political and had to be addressed and resolved politically.

Mong'are was a focused leader. He believed in making a promise when he was sure that he could accomplish it. I knew that if he promised to address the issue to its logical conclusion, he meant it. He teamed up with Senator John Kebaso and brought in old women who vowed to curse whoever was out to scuttle the establishment of Nyansiongo Secondary School.

At the time, the late James Nyamweya, then the MP for Nyaribari and member of Kenyatta's cabinet, had applied for Carnal Walkers' land. This is the exact place where Nyansiongo Secondary School (now Nyansiongo High School) is situated. As the issue of land troubled us, other opinions emerged. For instance, the people of Raitigo and Manga, who would end up being the first and direct beneficiaries of the school, claimed that the spot initially intended for the project (near Nyansiongo Primary School) was too far for them. They suggested that we find an alternative piece of land closer to them or shelve the plans we had. But for how long could we derail this important project that would benefit generations upon generations?

We had to find a way out. A delegation was dispatched to Nairobi to meet with Jackson Angaine who was the Minister for Lands and Settlement. He would receive an appeal to step in and assist us. This decision was arrived at after consultations amongst parents and advice from John Kebaso who was at the time the MP representing Borabu since the Senate had been abolished. This delegation, which I was part of, was led by Kebaso. Others in the team included David Oboso, Dishon Kengere and Jeremiah Mwambi. All these were committee members of my school, Nyansiongo DEB Primary School.

Details of this historic trip remain vivid in my mind. I recall that Senator Kebaso wore a cap made of leopard skin. This was probably a veiled signal that he was determined to win the battle ahead of us. At the meeting in Jackson Angaine's house, there was heat. This happened because the minister rejected the idea of approving our suggestion that we establish the secondary school on Carnal Walkers' land.

We were taken aback. Disappointed! It appeared that Kebaso was the most affected and was not going to accept the minister's decision. How could he lose in the presence of his voters? He shot up, raised his voice, and told the minister to either yield to the demands of the delegation or call President Jomo Kenyatta to arrest him. The minister appeared surprised by this turn of events. The trick worked! We had the last laugh when Angaine signed and issued the letter of allotment with which we could start the school project.

Back in Borabu, there was yet another hurdle! As indicated earlier, according to the people from Raitigo, the approved site was too far from them and they could not support it financially. For those from Manga, although the site was close to them, they said that they could not afford to implement it on their own. All this threw our plans into a spin once again!

I hardly give up on things that can transform people's lives. If I had this weakness, then I would have abandoned this challenging task at that stage. I kept pushing. I approached Chief Lawrence Sese and Assistant Chief Taratio Nyang'au and both bought into my plan. Accompanied by the two, we travelled to Kisii Town and headed straight to the headquarters of the SDA Conference in Nyanchwa. There, we made a request to the church to sponsor the school. I was disappointed once again, when the leadership led by Pastor Stanley Nyachieo declined, saying they did not have the requisite funds to meet the project's needs.

Our next attempt led us to Cardinal Otunga's office at Bishop Otunga (now Cardinal Otunga) High School-Mosocho. Bishop Otunga jumped on the idea of supporting the school as if he had been waiting for it. He was the Bishop of the Kisii Catholic Diocese. A few days later, he came to us with good news. He had paid for the land to the Settlement Fund Trustee. It was now all systems go for our pet project, building a secondary school at Nyansiongo.

The Catholic Church had a wider vision than we did at the time. Having acquired the land, the church envisioned turning Nyansiongo into a complex, with the establishment of a secondary school, a hospital and a university. At the time (1964), the area was under Ichuni Parish but Nyansiongo would attain the same status the following year.

Cardinal Otunga was a very strict and orderly person. He hit the ground running and, within no time, we had the first secondary school class at the white man's abandoned residence. The school admitted its first batch of students in 1966, with Fr Stupner Aloys on caretaker basis. According to the records at the Catholic Diocese of Kisii, the school has been led by seven principals since its inception. Peter Orendo who hailed from Western region was the first substantial head of the school. The Teachers' Service Commission seconded David Motanya who headed the school between 1970 and 1972 when he was succeeded by Vitalis Ojwando who headed the school up to 1975. The school was largely supported by the Catholic brothers at the initial stages. Its first premises were later converted to a dispensary which is in existence to date.

Since the school did not have a residence for teachers, we hosted Orendo at the primary school section for about two months. The two schools complemented each other, with the primary school having given the new one seed learners, with the help of the primary school committee before the new school got its own leadership.

As would be expected of any new project, there were teething problems at the new school. For instance, some learners were openly unruly. Orendo also lacked basics like food and proper accommodation within the school for efficient and round the clock management.

Although we had provided him with a place to stay in the primary school section, it was still dangerous for him to walk in a new place since the two schools were separated by a thick forest. To sort this hurdle, Mzee Yuvinalis Mocha offered to accommodate the teacher as we constructed a teacher's house in the secondary school compound. The house was ready after some months and he now settled in to execute his mandate as the pioneer headmaster of Nyansiongo Secondary School. Today, Nyansiongo High School stands out as one of the biggest and oldest learning institutions in Nyamira County.

*****

My love for starting schools was not confined to Borabu. Back in my original home, I was instrumental in the establishment of Nyabisimba Secondary School in 2006. The school sits at the top of the hill and part of it occupies my father's land. Mzee Ongaga Kinaro and my son Zablon were among those who joined me in initiating the school.

The institution is a product of a primary school with a similar name and the two are separated by a fence. It is interesting to note that part of the secondary school sits in Bogichora ward while the other is in Bonyamatuta. This is one of the co-shared resources by Abagichora and Abanyamatuta clans. It is a testimony that we are one people and when we come together, great things happen.

The need for the secondary school at Nyabisimba emanated from a request from the community. This was projected to increase the number of those who would transit from primary to secondary school. However, the available land at the time was not sufficient to accommodate the two institutions. When I learnt of this challenge from Kinaro, I convinced my family members for us to hive part of our father's land for the institution. In no time, I processed the title deed for the school. This paved way for the actualization of the project. The school is growing rapidly and receives students from Nyabisimba and the surrounding areas.

> **Biographer's Note:** Mzee Mabea's first son Zablon Agwata joined Nyansiongo Secondary School in 1972. At the time, it was headed by David Motanya.

In his recollection for the purposes of this story, Zablon said that at the time, the school had one stream for Forms 1-4. It also had two dormitories, one close to the tuition block while the other was across the road. The latter had been donated by the farmers' cooperative society and must have previously been used as a store and animal pen. A house that formerly belonged to a white settler served as the headmaster's office and staffroom, accounts office and the residence of the administrator.

"The school moved to its current location after 1975. When I joined, the school population was about 40 students. It lacked teachers in a number of subjects. In some subjects, we never saw a teacher before us. Nevertheless, we taught ourselves and passed our exams," Zablon said.

> **Biographer's Note:** Pr. Stanely Nyachieo who is mentioned in various sections of Mzee Mabea's story died shortly before we published this book. Mabea remembered him as a forthright honest and dedicated servant of the Lord and a role model to many in the community.

# When Corruption Fought Back

I noted earlier in this book that in the 1970s, 1980s and early 1990s, Kenya was leading the world in pyrethrum production. Indeed, according to an article published in *The East African* on November 13, 2018, Kenya produced an average 18,000 tonnes or 80 per cent of the world demand during those happy years. This earned the country 200 million Dollars in foreign exchange annually. When ills invaded the sector, pyrethrum production dropped drastically. Several societies collapsed and hundreds of thousands of Kenyan farmers, who relied on the crop, were thrown into the wallows of abject poverty.

The worst case happened in the present day Kisii and Nyamira counties where thousands of our people lost patience and uprooted the crop. Presently, one can hardly spot a pyrethrum farm in most constituencies in the two counties. This is despite the fact that pyrethrum was a major cash crop that was relied on by parents to raise fees for their children and empower themselves economically. Today, the world is more conscious of environmental issues and anecdotal reports suggest that the demand for organic insecticides may be going up! What an opportune time that would have been for pyrethrum growers in Kenya!

The same sad eventuality confronted the coffee sector.

Even with the collapse of the two sectors, hope was not lost. Local people embraced tea as a fall-back option and the crop has helped many to sustain their lives over the years. Like many people in Nyamira, part of my land is occupied with tea. Presently, Nyamira County alone has five tea factories serving the small scale tea farmers. However, the earnings from the crop have dwindled in recent years. This has been precipitated by poor crop husbandry practices, land subdivision to economically unviable portions, unclear and exploitative market trends, among other challenges.

To ensure that the same problems that crippled coffee and pyrethrum did not haunt tea, the Kenya Tea Development

Agency (KTDA) was created out of the Kenya Tea Development Authority that initially ran the affairs of the sector. In the new arrangement, farmers have representation at various levels, starting at the level of tea collection, all the way to the KTDA Board.

Soon after I retired, farmers in my zone which is affiliated to Nyansiongo Tea Factory elected me as their director. This happened due to my reputation as a forthright and dedicated person in my undertakings.

However, as soon as I got elected, I got into headwinds with my fellow directors. I was dismayed to learn that some had vested interests that blurred the interests and aspirations of the farmers. For instance, I learnt that there were unshakable cartels at the Mombasa Tea Auction depot that lived off farmers' sweat. Although it was clear that Nyansiongo Tea Factory produced high grade tea, the auctioneers sold it at throwaway prices.

I resolved to blow the whistle by sharing this information with my fellow directors, a move that made me very unpopular with some. Apparently, some of them were part of these cartels that needed to be weeded out. They were driven by selfish ambitions, colluding with the auctioneers to sell our produce at throwaway prices. In so doing, the directors in question drew handsome kickbacks. Using these proceeds from these dubious deals, they invested in private tea hawking companies which competed with the KTDA. Clearly, there was conflict of interest and their selfishness had blinded them from serving the farmers.

My concerns appeared to increasingly irk most of my colleague directors. Consequently, I felt isolated. This was worsened by the fact that, whenever I met the farmers who elected me, I enlightened them on market prices at the tea auction in Mombasa. Some directors were openly uncomfortable. They identified me as a 'betrayer', a person who should be alienated at all costs.

At the time, tea buying centres received road maintenance funds from the factories they fell under. The allocation was pegged on the cumulative produce of green tea bought from the farmers. Unlike some directors who meddled on the utilization of these funds, I let the Tea Buying Centre committees in my area of jurisdiction to run the kitty, while in close consultation with the Tea Leaf Manager. When this word went out, my fellow directors were annoyed. The move had cast them in bad light since they had interests in the award of road maintenance contracts in their zones. I was gradually becoming popular with farmers and unpopular in my fellow directors' faces.

Nevertheless, I chose to remain focused. I believed that tea had a future, but this depended on transparency at the auction. Above all, for our tea to compete favourably in the market, we had to improve quality and increase production by adopting new and high yielding varieties. Since individual farmers could not do it, they needed collective support from the factory, an undertaking that had financial implications. I knew that this was a noble idea but I had to approach it with circumspect, so that it would not boomerang due to prohibitive and (possibly) exaggerated costs. In our deliberations as factory directors and management, we were able to secure land where we established tea nurseries.

*****

Over time, experience has taught me that our people do not easily embrace new ideas, however worthwhile the ideas may be. Indeed, very few take risks. This slows down the uptake of viable initiatives and it has been our greatest undoing as a community and country.

For instance, after introducing the high yielding tea varieties in May 2001, I realized that many farmers were not keen to adopt them. This was partly due to the fact that uprooting what they already had in their farms was a labour intensive venture. Additionally, tea gets ready for harvest several years after it is planted. Worse still, many people hold their tea bushes 'emotionally' and special in a way. This is due to the manner in which it was introduced in Gusii back in the late 1950s through to 1960s. At the time of introducing the cash crop, the Tea Board of Kenya used to go to great lengths to vet and approve people who would venture into growing tea. This was a rigorous exercise and not many were approved. So, those who planted tea were highly regarded and saw themselves as special. Additionally, the crop was viewed with awe given the elaborate preparations prior to planting and the 'tender' care that followed to ensure there was no loss. Clearly, the farmers thought it was wiser staying with the existing tea bushes instead of planting new ones.

This is the understanding that compelled me to select twelve young men from my area and take them to Kericho, where they could benchmark on best crop husbandry practices. I expected them to learn how proper tea nurseries were established and taken care of. Once in Kericho, which is the renowned tea producer closer to my area, the youthful farmers were guided on tea nursery establishment and other husbandry practices. Through the networks I had made in Kericho, I obtained a nursery establishment permit and plastic containers that the youths would use to apply the skills they had learnt to establish nurseries at home.

Once back home, I encouraged those that had been trained to expand their networks and bring others on board. Using the nursery establishment permit, I bought several seeds for them with which they produced thousands of shoots. They then transplanted them in their farms and sold the rest. This way, farmers in Ekware, Nyamasibi, Kenyenya and Esise started growing new and vibrant tea varieties.

This caused discomfort in some directors yet again. There was also disquiet from their people that the directors were sleeping on the job. Although the directors did not confront me to disclose their reservations, I gathered from their close associates that they felt that my actions would undermine and cost them their positions in the long-run.

*****

While I served as tea factory director, another memorable thing happened. A Chinese investor came with intentions of helping farmers establish a one-line factory that would process green tea. A one line factory is a smaller model that is less expensive than the ones installed by the KTDA. I managed to create a forum for the investor at Riang'ombe Tea Buying Centre where he spoke to the farmers. The meeting was fruitful and the farmers got ready and willing to adopt the idea.

The investor was excited just as I was. However, our excitement was short-lived. Some of my colleague directors and the factory management had got wind of the deliberations from the meeting and vowed to scuttle the resolutions. These opponents moved with speed and wrote to the KTDA Headquarters, urging the top management to warn the Chinese investor to keep off. When he got wind of court threats, the investor fled the country and the idea aborted.

As this was happening, I was serving as the Vice Chairman of Nyansiongo Tea Factory. When elections for Gesima electoral area were held, the late James Ombui who was my chairman was defeated. Constitutionally, I was supposed to take over as the chairman but this never happened. As soon as the elections were over, dark forces in the factory ganged up against me and vowed to make sure that I would never rise to the position of chairman. As a result, the factory operated without a substantive chairman for nearly three months. With the KTDA management having taken sides to my disadvantage, I made it clear that I was not interested in the chairmanship and was comfortable discharging my duties as the grower's representative and vice-chairman.

Although we cut an image of a united force, it was often a case of fireworks during the directors' meetings. I had made a commitment never to let any malpractice happen under my watch, something that really isolated me further from some of my colleagues. In the run-up to elections for my electoral area, they teamed up with one tea auctioneer from Nairobi and campaigned against me using their underhand networks. Despite this, I won with a landslide, to their chagrin.

In spite of my win, it did not take many days before I discovered that I was not out of the woods yet. My opponents had gone back to the drawing board to cut me to size and forces at a higher level played ball. In the strategy, a clause was introduced at the KTDA Headquarters that anyone who was aged 60 years and above was not qualified to be elected as a director. I was 62 at the time and I had just been elected. However, I had not been sworn into office as the factory guidelines provided. Using this criterion from KTDA, I was barred from assuming the position of director. My directorship career in the tea sector ended! Just like that!

However, from the foregoing, it is evident that the issues I was raising as a director were in the best interest of the people I represented. Our tea continues to do poorly in the international market. In recent years, prices have nosedived and left farmers lamenting that they are in a venture that is not rewarding and commensurate to their sweat. The downward plunge of prices can be addressed if we embrace value addition at our factories. Tea hawking continues to rival structured selling by the KTDA, an outfit that has equally not effectively run the business. To this date and age, our farmers spend endless time at the buying centers, waiting to sell their green leaves. In the process, the produce withers and quality gets compromised. The farmers end up getting proceeds that are not proportional to their sweat. These are emotive issues that need to be fixed if the tea sector is to thrive.

> ***Editor's Note:*** *At the time of writing this book, there was an ongoing outcry in the Kenyan press regarding the conduct of the KTDA. The agency was accused of imposing undue control of the sector, conflict of interest, among other accusations. The result is that the farmer gets the 'short end of the stick'. As a result the Cabinet Secretary for Agriculture, Peter Munya, issued a set of guidelines for the agency. He also vowed to effect reforms that may impact on the manner in which the agency runs the sector.*

## Mecheo Location is Created

Before the Constitution of Kenya 2010 was promulgated, Kenya had a Provincial Administration structure. Through this model, the government had representatives right from the grassroots to the national level. At the lowest level, there were sub-locations which were headed by the Assistant Chief. Up the ladder, we had locations, divisions, districts and eight provinces. These were headed by the Chief, Division Officer, District Commissioner and the Provincial Commissioner, respectively.

The present day Nyamira County fell under Nyanza Province. The province was headquartered in Kisumu. Apart from Nyanza, there were seven other provinces that made up the country. These were: Rift Valley, Central, North Eastern, Eastern, Western, Coast and Nairobi. It was through these administrative structures that the Presidency was felt from Nairobi to every part of the country.

The 47 counties we have today took the boundaries of districts that were created in the 1990s. Before devolution took effect, the present day Nyamira County had five districts namely, Borabu, Masaba North, Nyamira North, Nyamira South and Masaba South. All these were amalgamated based on constituency boundaries and called sub-counties which form Nyamira County.

In Borabu District, we had three divisions, several locations and sub locations. Specifically, my location Esise which comprised of Raitigo, Manga and Magombo settlement schemes was represented by one chief.

In our informal thinking as residents, we felt that the area was too expansive to be represented by one chief. Our feeling was that Esise location deserved to be a division of its own with two or more locations.

But the incumbent administrator in the larger location was not playing ball, or so we thought. For reasons best known to him, it appeared that the chief was opposed to the idea that some of us were nursing. Over time, we discovered that the administrator did not want the location to be divided as this would reduce his influence and downscale his other personal interests.

Several meetings were held and numerous memoranda written, but there were no fruits forthcoming. Although a majority of people from my area including Zed Ondari, Stephen Ogechi and Samuel Omosa supported the idea, there were a few who enjoyed a close-knit friendship with the chief. The chief's buddies wielded influence and were not ashamed of siding with him whenever he pursued an agenda that had little or no meaningful impact on the people. For instance, whenever the chief handled land dispute cases, he would make unfair judgments and get away with it. I was a victim of this unfair treatment by the chief when I was confronted with a boundary dispute with one of my neighbours.

When he changed his mind to support the creation of a new location, the chief proposed that it be created with boundaries stretching from Ekware at Nyaribari Masaba Matunwa, Manga Township bordering Kineni Location, all the way to Harambee to the Sotik West border. For some of us, this formed a long and shapeless location that did not take into account parameters like population size and composition. However, the chief received overwhelming support from his friends since the proposal favoured them in the short term. Despite the disquiet from some of us, the chief hurriedly said that our proposal did not make sense. We were shocked because he did not subject the matter to a vote or further discussion. To defeat fairness, he handpicked a few individuals whom he could manipulate and they went public to support his idea of creating Manga location.

Soon, a divisional meeting was held. On the material day, tension was evident in the air as time for the meeting approached. As the meeting that was presided over by the chief and attended by the DO got underway, a number of people including myself repeatedly raised hands to air our opinions about the unpopular proposal but we were out rightly ignored. It appeared that, although the chief was subordinate to the DO, he either had his blessings to armtwist the attendees or he overlooked his boss.

Tempers rose as time elapsed. I resolved to confront the DO and tell him to his face that he was doing disservice to us by allowing his junior to push his agenda down our throats. "Sit down or leave this meeting," the DO shot back. I could not give in.

I knew I had the backing of a good number of people in the meeting and nobody would harm or cow me down. Therefore, amid the hullabaloo, I aired my views. As I advanced my opinion, those who had been jeering went quiet and I went on to speak for nearly twenty minutes. In my speech, I kept my eyes on the DO most of the time and I could tell that he was keenly listening.

I did not resume my seat after speaking. Instead, I took a vehicle to Kisii Town in search of water tight evidence to pursue the matter further. The journey took me about two hours. Once in town, I proceeded to the Lands Surveyor's office and made a polite request to buy copies of maps of Esise Location/Division. The officer granted the request and after availing the copies to me, I arranged them neatly and left the office.

*****

The following day, I called a few people who were not happy with the manner the issue was being handled by the chief. Those present and who were at the forefront in pushing for fairness included Ogechi, Omosa and Ondari. In our meeting, we went through the memorandum that the administrator had made while disregarding our views. After lengthy deliberations, we wrote a counter-memorandum to the Permanent Secretary in the Office of the President, Mutea Iringo. In it, we indicated what we needed and how the chief had meddled in the affair to satisfy his whims. Once done, I went home satisfied that I had the arsenal that would quash the chief's selfish agenda and we could get our way.

The next day, evening darkness found me on my way to Metamaywa trading centre where I took a night bus destined for Nairobi. Once in the city, I freshened up and headed straight to Mutea Iringo's office where I arrived at 8 am. Although I had not booked an appointment with him, I had resolved to try my luck and have a word with him. By the time I was ushered into the secretary's office, there were several people at the waiting bay. Aside from me, they were all booked to see the PS and were looking forward to be attended by him.

From the look of things, I was not going to see the PS. According to the secretary, her boss was only seeing those who had appointments with him. This got me worried. I had covered several kilometres in the interest of hundreds of people from my area. I knew if I went back without seeing the PS, it would negate the agenda we had vowed to pursue. So, I prayed to God to make it possible for me to accomplish my aspirations that morning.

That day, I was smartly dressed. I had my best suit and necktie on. A badge of honour that I had received from the Nile Basin due to my dedication to avail clean water in my area rested on my lapel. I had received the badge during a high-powered weeklong seminar in Dar es Salaam, Tanzania, which was attended by delegates from ten countries. As I meditated in the PS's waiting bay, I panned my eyes to the door and saw him walk in. This raised my heartbeat instantly. Everyone looked up as the PS waved at us and entered his office.

Minutes later, the secretary came to me and requested to take my badge. I promptly obliged and she took it straight to her boss who then told her that he would attend me first. As I entered the expansive office with sophisticated furniture, I thanked God for answering my prayer that I had made minutes ago.

"Your name does not sound new. Are you related to Lands Commissioner Zablon Mabea or District Commissioner Mabea?" PS Iringo asked me not long after I sat in the chair that he had ushered me into.

"Yes, the Lands Commissioner is my son and the DC is related to me from my maternal side," I told him.

"Are you going to introduce me to your son or I should introduce you to him," he went on, smiling.

"If you introduce me, it may take long. Let me introduce you to him," I answered, to which he laughed lightly and told me to go ahead.

I took my phone, dialled Zablon's number and he took the call immediately. After exchanging greetings, I told my son that I was with a friend who wanted to greet him and he allowed me to pass the phone to the PS. In their talk, the PS introduced himself and sought to know from my son if I had a problem that needed his intervention. This surprised Zablon, who was not aware that I had travelled to the city. He assured the PS that I was capable of expressing myself satisfactorily even without his intervention.

"Have you had your breakfast," PS Iringo asked me as soon as I disengaged the phone and I responded, "no, I did not have time. I will do so after leaving your office." He then ordered his secretary to bring us tea as we conversed.

I told him that the problem that had made me travel was communal and I was a messenger. As I explained myself, his facial expressions indicated that he was shocked with the revelations I was making to him concerning his officers at the grassroots. I further told him that since I was at the forefront in agitating for fairness in the creation of new locations, I had become a marked person by those resistant to the idea.

As our talk got underway, I showed the PS copies of the chief's memorandum and the other one originating from residents of Mecheo for comparison. It emerged that, although we had sent such correspondences to his office before, they never reached him. Interestingly, he had seen the communications from the chief concerning the matter. I made it clear to him that the information originating from the chief was unpopular on the ground and that I was the one who deposited the residents' letters at the G4S courier services at Keroka and retained the receipts. From the look of things, the letters never reached his office and there was a possibility that someone ensured they never did.

The PS read a few pages then indicated that he wanted to call the junior staff, a suggestion I politely encouraged him to ignore. Tea was ready and as we consumed it, he closely scrutinized the earlier memoranda. I pleaded with him never to reveal to anyone that I had travelled to his office to pursue this matter that was hot back home. The PS appeared taken and consumed in the documents. Time was running fast and the people in the queue were getting impatient. Since he had decided to address my issue conclusively, he told the secretary to give the visitors a different date.

The PS moved everything on his table aside, and then spread the maps I had taken from the lands office in Kisii. While he paid keen interest, I showed him the boundaries of the location as proposed by the chief and those in our proposal. He was evidently shocked with the chief's proposal, saying that it was a narrow strip of land covering almost twenty miles. He then said that the proposal emanating from the people made sense and could be adopted by his office.

As I folded the maps to return them into my bag, the PS took his desk phone and made a call. I could not tell whom he was talking to but as their conversation advanced, I learnt that the person on the other end was not a stranger to me. I could tell that they were discussing the two maps that I had brought to the office and the recipient was agreeing that the chief had done disservice by forwarding a proposal that his people had rejected. From my eavesdropping, I could tell that the recipient was someone on the ground. Although the phone distorted the voice for me to clearly tell whose it was, the person on the other end was telling the PS that he knew me and we always consulted back home. The person told him that I was a dependable and principled person and my plan had the blessings of the people and should be adopted.

When they finished talking, the PS decided to call in a junior officer to assist me to capture some important requirements that would make the process of creating Mecheo Location possible. But when he mentioned the name of the officer, I told him immediately that I did not have faith in him. I elaborated to the PS that the officer he had in mind was the same person I suspected to have diverted our letters from reaching his office. To deliver my claims home, I showed the PS the receipts from the G4S Keroka office addressed to the officer. We had been using the officer in trust because he hailed from our community, not knowing that he was a relative of the chief who was using him to scuttle our plans.

The PS was petrified. He wanted to call the officer and shame him but I advised him not to do so. I further told him that I did not want the officer to know that I was in Nairobi pursuing the matter because I was afraid he would pass the information back home. This was likely to throw me deeper into a collision path with the administrator. Convinced, the PS called in another officer by the name Achoki whom he gave firm instructions to assist me. Achoki took me to his office where we spent the better part of the afternoon, scrutinizing issues like population size fit for a location, the number of schools and markets in the area, among others.

I left the office after Achoki had guided me on how to fill the forms and having agreed to return them to the PS the following morning fully filled. In my presence, the PS directed Achoki to run with the matter until the new location got gazetted. The PS also called the DC Borabu, Mohammed Nur Hassan, and instructed him on what to do within specified timelines and without fail. I left the office a happy and hopeful man.

Back home, I assured the community that I had delivered their message and that I had obtained assurance that we will have a new location. We all started a countdown for the day the news will be broken to us, so that we could celebrate together. It did not take long. In a week's time, we received news that Mecheo Location had been gazetted with two sub-locations, Matunwa and Endemu. Achoki sent me copies of the gazette notice which I happily presented to the DC Borabu who was equally elated that the matter had reached a logical conclusion.

The DC then swiftly embarked on establishing the location by making public pronouncements about it. He consulted with the people and we told him that we needed the new location to be operationalized so that we could harvest the fruits of our sweat. Soon, he appointed Charles Karaya who was the Assistant Chief for Manga sub location to be the Acting Chief of the new location. Before long, the posts of Chief for Mecheo location and Assistant Chiefs for Endemu and Matunwa were advertised. People thought since I had been at the forefront to have the administrative units created, I could have a hand in the recruitment of their pioneer administrators. However, I had chosen to stay away from the exercise, lest it tainted my image.

Even with the presence of an acting chief, some doubting 'Thomases' existed. They argued that the location was only on paper and did not exist on the ground. They claimed that the Acting Chief Charles Karaya did not have an office and he was serving people along the paths. To silence them, I rented a resident's shop at Sh1,000 a month and turned it into a temporary office for the chief. Additionally, a friend bought some chairs, a shelf and table for the chief. When the people saw this, their doubts flew through their windows.

As I noted, the use of this office was a temporary measure. We reasoned that a chief is a government officer and should not operate from a private premise for long. Therefore, we embarked on resource mobilization, urging the community to donate a piece of land where the chief's office could be built. The people of Mecheo had suffered for long, going for government services at Esise which was quite far.

Now that the chief's office was near them, they owned the new location fully. In so doing, we consulted amongst ourselves and found a piece of land for the office. The office now sits on a piece of land that is large enough for government activities at that level. However, we are yet to have offices for the two assistant chiefs.

How the first Kerina pyrethrum society looked like at Kenyenya.

This building in Kisii Town belongs to Kerina Cooperative Society.

Nyabisimba Secondary School sign post.

Nyabisimba Secondary School. Part of the school sits on our family land.

Riamabea SDA Church built on land that my family donated.

A closer picture of Riamabea SDA Church built on land that my family donated.

The old and new church buildings are sandwitched in trees.

Mecheo SDA Church. A new structure is coming up near it.

A water kiosk built at Mecheo market. Four such kiosks exist in our area..

Entrance to Mecheo High School. There is a primary school with the same name nearby..

Endemu dam that has been encroached.

Some world heads of state who attended the Dar event.

Sitting second right is myself following proceedings during the Dar event.

I took this photo in the sidelines of the World Water Day-Nile Initiative in Dar, Tanzania.

Here, I am walking with hands in the pocket alongside other delegates during the water conference in Dar.

Construction of Metamaywa-Chepng'ombe Road.

I am standing second left with foreign friends in Dar.

Part of the tarmacked road near Metamaywa.

With Richard Wang who is part of the team constructing a murram road in my area.

Directors of Nyansiongo Tea Factory, among them Kegoro (a former MP) & Nyagarama (now Governor of Nyamira County)

I'm seated third right in this group photo taken at the Sunset Hotel, Kisumu in 2009.

I am standing to the right of President Uhuru Kenyatta when he was installed as Gusii elder.. With me in the photo are some pastors and mmembers of the Gusii Council of Elders.

# Church Matters

From the onset, I indicated that I was born to parents who subscribed to the Christian faith. Specifically, my parents were Seventh Day Adventists (SDAs). They brought me up to love and fear God as the Creator of the universe, the Giver and Protector of life. Since my childhood, I have walked this path of Christianity and I do not have any intentions, whatsoever, of deviating from the teachings of my denomination.

Although I am a sinner, I believe that my parents were right when they introduced me to Christianity. Surely, they did their part as captured in the book of Proverbs 22:6 which says that, "Start the children off on the way they should go, and even when they are old they will not turn from it." - *New International Version.*

From as early as the age of 10, I was active in church matters. While learning at Motagara Intermediate School, I was tasked to be the youth leader at Kenyenya SDA Church. At the time, churches were a fair distance apart. However, this was never an excuse for one to skip church functions. Accompanied by my fellow youths, we could walk long distances for church gatherings. I vividly recall that we never saw it difficult walking from our home areas to Ogango Camp Centre in Kitutu Masaba constituency, to be spiritually nourished. This journey was about 30 km and we covered it on foot to and fro.

The annual weeklong camp meetings at Ogango attracted the faithful from all corners of Gusii. Some would stay there the whole week, worshiping in prayer, singing and doing bible study day and night. This was despite the fact that the church did not have permanent buildings. The faithful built small grass-thatched huts *(ebigutu)* where they stayed for the entire camping period. They came in with their food and shared it amongst themselves, a thing that is no longer there these days. Pastor Abraham Oirere was one of the most eloquent preachers stationed at Ogango those days.

In the 1960s and 1970s, church members exhibited a high level of commitment to Christianity. They were focused on preaching the gospel, bringing in new converts and having them baptized, in preparation for the second coming of Jesus the Saviour. Due to this commitment exhibited by church leaders and members, the church population grew quickly. After some years, another camp centre was opened at Kebirigo. This was nearer home and cut the distance we covered previously by almost six times.

When I graduated from college and became a teacher, it did not take three years before I moved my station for spiritual services to Raitigo Camp Centre. While working as a teacher at Nyansiongo Primary School, I always found time for the Lord. In the SDA teachings, Saturday is a day of rest. Even if you were busy through the week, you have to dedicate the day to worshiping God. I always wished that I could give church matters adequate time but the nature of my profession and responsibilities as the headmaster never allowed me.

However, I played a critical role in the acquisition of a plot for Mecheo SDA Church. Being the headmaster of Nyansiongo Primary School, I was well known in most parts of Borabu. Additionally, my home is not far from where Mecheo SDA Church stands today. When the need arose for the church to be established, members had hectic time finding a suitable plot for its location. Pastor Stanley Nyachieo, who was my teacher at Motagara Intermediate School, had risen to become the manager of schools sponsored by the Nyanchwa SDA Conference. Our paths crossed again and we became formidable buddies. Pr Nyachieo had also moved base to the settlement scheme and acquired a piece of land at a place currently called Entubokia. Although the piece of land was small, this is where the pastor had decided to settle before luck struck his door once again and he got another piece at Matutu where he ultimately settled.

Before Pr Nyachieo left Entubokia, I met him and made a request that we acquire a plot where we could build a church. Being a man of God, it did not need me to belabour the point so as to convince him. He promptly agreed that a church was a priority in the area and a search for the plot started in earnest. Even so, the two of us were worried of accomplishing the task because we did not have any money with which we could purchase the land the moment we got it.

As alluded to previously, this is how we agreed that Pr Nyachieo would approach his cousin Paul Nyachieo. Paul was at the time the Clerk of the Gusii County Council. He had helped us purchase Plot P1 (332) for Mecheo SDA School. The church stands on part of the land that previously belonged to the school.

At the time of the purchase, some people had encroached on the land. These people did not want to leave freely and this caused them trouble. Police were called in and they arrested them. However, over time, the entire land P1 (332) became a property of the church. This is the church where I presently fellowship.

*****

My retirement from teaching in 1995 coincided with a crisis at Mecheo SDA School and Church. It emerged that some people in the area did not want to recognize the school as sponsored by the SDA Church. At the centre of this was the ownership of the land on which the school and church stood. To resolve the crisis that was threatening to get ugly, I travelled to Kisii Town and headed straight to the Gusii County Council offices where I managed to obtain a receipt that was issued by the Settlement Trust Fund as proof that the land, title P1 (332), was a property of the SDA Church. Apparently, some people had illegally and secretly attempted to change the ownership of the property from the church to the community. With the evidence from the council, the name of the institution, right from the signpost were changed to indicate that the school was an SDA-sponsored institution.

In due course, the church leadership thought it wise to have the church that was under the head eldership of Jemima Otieno secure a title for its 'own' land. This would enable the church expand in line with the Nyamira SDA Conference guidelines. Members of the church knew how well-versed

I was concerning acquisition of land documents and they requested me to help the church elder in fast-tracking the process. We resolved to do the demarcation and acquisition of title deeds for the three institutions (Mecheo SDA Church, Mecheo Primary School and Mecheo Secondary School) that sat on the land P1 (332). Logically, this was cheaper and would seal gaps for any unforeseeable conflicts in future.

The land board for Borabu was in place. We submitted a formal request to the board to allow us sub-divide the land and it was granted. This elated church members and restored their confidence that they now legally owned the plot where the church stood.

The acquisition of the title deed for Mecheo SDA Church appeared to have set the precedence for other churches in the area to pursue the document. As a result, leaders from those churches approached me seeking guidance on how to go about the matter that had eluded them for a long time. Subsequently, this need for title deeds informed the decision of the pastor in charge of Mecheo Pastoral District and other leaders to appoint me as the chairman of the Church Development Committee in the district.

With this mandate resting on me, we managed to pursue and acquire title deeds for Tindereti, Kenyerere, Ribwago and Keginga SDA churches. Along the way, we came across an obstacle while pursuing the land documents for churches under Keginga Camp Centre. This happened as a result of internal conflicts pitying a section of church elders who in turn misled the pastor to abandon the idea midway. This discord reversed the strides churches like Matunwa and Endemu had made in a bid to obtain the important property ownership documents.

All along, I have been steadfast in church matters. This has seen me hold a number of leadership positions at Mecheo SDA Church where I fellowship. For instance, while heading the Church Development Committee, there emerged growing concern amongst members that the church was surrounded by thick bushes and shrubs. This provided a safe abode for snakes that often scared children on their way to or from church. Children were also uncomfortable taking their Sabbath School lessons in the open as is the tradition in SDA churches found in the countryside. To address the challenge, there was need to build a shelter for the young worshippers.

In one discussion in church, this matter cropped up. As it was being discussed, my son Zablon Agwata who had come home for a visit and was present keenly listened. A man of few words, Zablon never uttered a word. However, his heart was in consonance with members' sentiments. After the meeting, he quietly gave his personal donation to elder Isaac Nyamweya and encouraged him to spearhead the construction of the structure.

When elder Nyamweya disclosed the information to the church the next Sabbath, members were elated and equally encouraged. It was then agreed that since the existing church building had developed cracks, it needed attention as well. It would also look awkward if we started a minor structure for the children while the main church stood with open cracks. Therefore, it was resolved that as church members, we should make a sacrifice and devote ourselves to start putting up a modern building that would have partitions for offices and Sabbath School classes.

The church nominated elder Nyamweya and me and tasked us to reach out to my son Zablon with yet another request. We told him to help us get an architectural design for a structure suitable to accommodate children study rooms, the main church and offices. He promptly promised to get back to us. A few days later, he sent Eng. Joel Bwonda (also a member of our church) to us and after taking him to the site, the architect promised to send us preliminary designs that we would study and adopt or suggest any amendments. True to his word, he sent us the building plan and never asked for any money for the service.

When the building plan was shown to church members, they were happy. They all approved it without suggesting any changes to be made. Members were re-energized and ready to undertake this project for the Lord. My son Zablon was among the key initiators and to kick start the project, he contributed iron bars worth Sh375,000.

When the foundation and ground of the building got finished, problems started. There was outright interference by some church elders who brought in confusion. They defied the need for consulting engineers regularly to monitor the progress of the building. In their mission that was aimed at cutting costs and finishing the project quickly, they appeared to have thrown quality concerns through the window. They could buy substandard materials and go ahead to have it used by the masons. This has in the long run derailed the project that would have been completed a long time ago.

Perhaps this is where our people go wrong. When you have been entrusted with a responsibility on behalf of God and mankind, there is need for you to execute it with all honesty and diligence. It is not proper to ignore experts, more especially when undertaking a project that has implications on people's safety and is worth millions of shillings, marshalled by the people. There is no way one can ignore the advice of construction engineers from the County Government and the National Environmental Management Authority (NEMA) when undertaking a massive project like a storey church building.

The law dictates that, while undertaking such a project, experts must be involved at every step. There should be a duplicate book where the engineers can sign after assessing the progress of the project. Essentially, the church building committee should ensure that it follows the law of the land to the letter. This is for the good and safety of those who will use the facility in future. Indeed, many of the buildings that collapse in the country do so because they were shoddily done. However, I pray that God intervenes and we finish this ambitious project successfully and we will glorify His name.

This setback aside, I recall that six years ago, church members wished to have a public address system. They sent me to my son Zablon with a request for him to support us. When I did, Zablon brought the machine that he bought from the city. The public address system has been very instrumental in spreading the gospel.

Earlier, I had donated a cupboard and a number of books to the church. I also managed to get a large sheet that we use to partition the church into two during Passovers. This is not much but I wish I could do more for the Lord who has been so good to me and my family all along. I will continue doing His work as long as I am alive. I pray that we lead an honest life for this will draw us closer to God.

*****

In the life we lead on earth, one can traverse the world but never forget where he came from. Indeed, to me, I believe that home is best. This is why I have retained strong bonds with my larger family back home where my umbilical cord was disposed. I noted earlier that I built a semi-permanent house there, the first of its kind in the area. It stands to date.

However, the house is not as dear to my heart as Riamabea SDA Church is. This is a house of the Lord that stands on part of the land that I inherited from my father. To some extent, I think the project would not have come into being were it not that my mother and her co-wives were born again Christians. But again, God's plans surpass my understanding and I could be wrong in my assertion.

My version is that my mother and step-mothers previously fellowshipped at Embonga SDA Church. With time, the membership in that church grew and a need arose to divide them. A Sabbath School was started at Nyabisimba hilltop, the only place that space could be found at the time. Since the mothers' houses were at the foot of the hill, they found it cumbersome to climb and descend the hill every Saturday.

It was a challenge exacerbated as they advanced in age. They had increasingly grown old and feeble to the extent that they could sit at home on Saturdays instead of attending church as it had been their norm. However, this decision of literally 'boycotting' church unsettled their hearts. Then one day, they called me home and I availed myself.

When I arrived, they were seated under a fruit tree, absorbed in a conversation that made it difficult for them to notice me from far. When they saw me, their faces lit up with smiles that flattened the wrinkles on their faces. We exchanged greetings and without wasting time, they told me that they had stopped attending church because of the steep and uneven terrain.

I walked with them and crossed the road to the lower side of my piece of land, then made a stop where there were low lying bushes. "Can you manage to reach here every Saturday?" I asked them and they all responded in the affirmative. They then put their knees down, one by one and I followed suit. My mother prayed and asked God to sanctify the spot. True to their prayers, Riamabea SDA Church now conspicuously stands at the place. This happened because when my son Zablon got the news of the plan, he was very supportive and happy. To build the house of the Lord, Zablon mobilized his cousins and other young people in the area to raise funds. Zablon's uncle Surumo Bonyi is among those who took a notably active role in supporting the project. He argued that it could not be left to Zablon alone who had injected the initial amount. I also facilitated the acquisition of a title deed for the quarter acre piece of land to the church for Nyamira SDA Conference to accept it as one of its babies. God has been good to us and the church is reaching out to souls. A number of people in the neighbourhood who led lives away from the church have since been baptized and taken leadership positions in the church.

# Peace Keeping

I was born and brought up at a time when human life was greatly cherished. Violence was greatly abhorred at the family and community level. However, peace and tranquility could be occasionally stirred at the family level when men bartered their wives or when a conflict emerged concerning the sharing of resources, especially land. These cases were often nipped in the bud before they could escalate and cause bloodshed.

At the community level, issues like cattle theft were common. In Borabu, for example, we often became victims of this out-dated and retrogressive practice. Raiders could strike in the dead of the night and drive away the animals across the border to the Rift Valley side. On a lucky night, victims could raise alarm and neighbours could respond and repulse the rustlers. On an unlucky occasion, the raiders could get away with the animals. In other incidents, there ensued a confrontation that led to loss of life or injuries. Presently, there are several people in Borabu who live with arrow scars. Many others were rendered paupers after all their herds were taken by the heartless thieves.

As a senior citizen, I can confirm that the 2007/08 post-election violence was the worst experience Kenya ever encountered. The conflict was precipitated by a disputed outcome of the presidential poll. In the orgy of violence, many innocent Kenyans were flushed out of their homes and killed while several others were internally displaced. The worst hit by the chaos were members of communities who were perceived to be 'foreigners' in parts of the Rift Valley which was the hotspot of the violence. For instance, in Borabu, Nyachieng'a Ondara was butchered at the height of the violence.

Movement was a challenge. Roads were barricaded by blood thirsty gangs armed with crude weapons. They lit bonfires, looted shops and homes and also indiscriminately raped women. Due to the mess, essential goods would not be delivered to markets. The violence in Kenya grabbed the headlines globally, with the international media relaying images from Nairobi which suggested that Kenya was burning. Broadly saying, Kenya walked on a thin thread and I was afraid that the country would plunge into a full-blown civil war. I wondered why Kenya, known over time as the home of peace in a troubled continent, was quickly degenerating into a banana republic. Indeed, we nearly lost the country due to tribalism that overshadowed a political process that had equally been mishandled by the defunct Electoral Commission of Kenya (ECK). At a personal level, I got troubled and prayed without stopping. I was worried because my place is not far from the Rift Valley-Nyanza common border where there were frequent flare-ups at the time. Many people lost their property while others were killed. Still others fled with their lives from places like Kericho, Bomet, Nakuru, Uasin Gishu and Kitale. These were the epicentre of the chaos. Those who managed to flee the orgy of violence were either accommodated in temporary camps or in their relatives' homes. I heaved a sigh of relief when God calmed the storm, using Africa's eminent persons namely, Koffi Annan, Benjamin Mkapa and Graca Machel. These great Africans managed to prevail on Mwai Kibaki and his challenger in the race, Raila Odinga, to put Kenya ahead of their personal interests.

*****

When I retired from teaching, I retreated to my home and got concerned with the stories I was getting. For instance, I learnt that some families were having unending quarrels over land boundaries and could even resort to physical fights. Some of these confrontations, many of which involved children of the people who migrated there, ended tragically with the loss of lives.

I noted earlier that Borabu was initially settled by white settlers. When they exited, the land was sold to people who came in from various parts of Gusii. These people have converted the area into a cosmopolitan settlement as no single clan dominates. However, I got saddened that some young people did not understand the vision their parents had when they bought land in Borabu. They could not put themselves in the shoes of their parents who sacrificed their all, took loans that they serviced the whole of their lives, to purchase the land. Due to this outright ignorance, the young generation either mismanaged or haphazardly sold the properties that were meant to better their lives at throw-away prices.

Further, due to old age or death, some families experienced problems when it came to subdivision of land for inheritance purposes. This led to serious animosity that threatened to claim lives. Worse yet, and this is unfortunate, some neighbours who should have taken the role of arbiters fuelled family conflicts. Instead of helping to resolve the emerging rifts, they took sides as families got fragmented. Some of these disputes ignited massive temperatures and it appeared that some civil servants in the defunct provincial administration were beneficiaries of the prevailing scenario.

Using wisdom and dialogue skills, I diligently managed to settle some of these cases at the affected families' level. For instance, one family had taken the battle to the court of law, using thousands upon thousands of shillings to pursue justice. I managed to bring them to the negotiation table and they agreed to withdraw the case and settle the matter at home.

In the same spirit and due to the experience I had gained during my days as a teacher and education administrator, I was able to bring a number of adversaries to the dialogue table and make them understand the significance of reconciliation and peaceful co-existence. When the brothers who, for a long time, could not see eye to eye reconciled, I was very happy. I had taken a risk by encouraging them to withdraw the case from court. Had I failed to solve it with them, I would have found myself part of their mess. I got even happier when I learnt that the now reconciled brothers were proudly telling the world that the dispute that had distanced them for years was now water under the bridge, courtesy of my intervention.

My decision to discourage people from pursuing land matters in court was informed by the fact that neighbours understand the boundaries and cultural issues better than the courts do. Further, in court, the winner takes it all while at home the warring parties reach a win-win situation when the matter is solved. A court of law may solve a case but leave the parties divided even more.

To me, I believe that people of the same lineage should not take their battles to the courts; not unless other right mechanisms like dialogue at home have failed. In our traditional society, we had effective mediation mechanisms that assured justice for all. Further, justice focused more on remedy than punishment and elders always balanced between 'winning' and family/community harmony.

When the brothers reconciled and shared the news of their restored peace, I received a flood of similar requests. A good number of families that were entangled in a similar mess wanted to engage me to help them resolve it amicably. They endeared themselves to me further because I helped in the mediation at no cost.

*****

I cannot tell how information about my operations reached some peace-keeping organizations that did not have offices anywhere near my home. Such organizations included Uwiano/Platform for Peace Keeping. One time when this organization put up a forum in Nairobi, I was invited to attend. As I came to suspect, Jacqueline Mogeni who hails not far from my home, must have proposed my name to the forum organizers.

I attended the meeting at the 14$^{th}$ floor of Bruce House along Standard Street, Nairobi, on September 21$^{st}$, 2017. Accompanying me from Kisii was Protus Nyansera, Maati Ooga and Edward Bikundo. Primarily, the meeting sought to find out what caused conflicts at family and community levels. Delegates were also expected to consolidate peace and reconciliation processes in the country.

The meeting was addressed by various people including Jacqueline Mogeni who was the Chief Executive Officer; Wafula Chebukati, Chairman of the Independent Electoral and Boundaries Commission (IEBC); Mkenya Daima founder and trustee, Vimal Shah; the Media Council of Kenya's former Chief Executive Officer Haron Mwangi and the NCIC Chairman, Francis Ole Kaparo. Others were former Inspector General of Police, Joseph Boinett; Registrar of Political Parties, Lucy Ndung'u; Piece Net Kenya Chief Executive Officer, Sam Oando; United Nations Development Programme (UNDP) Country Director, Amanda Summaga and the UN-Women Country Director, Zebib Kavuma.

In the meeting, several suggestions were advanced on how Kenya could reduce tensions that erupt in the run-up, during and immediately after general elections. It was agreed that there should be intensified peace campaigns prior, during and after elections. We agreed that everyone should be an ambassador of peace.

Further, the meeting was given a picture of what transpired in previous elections. They looked at Nyanza region as a case study. They looked at Luo Nyanza and Gusii (Nyamira and Kisii) and evaluated the way the two regions had reacted to the post-election violence of 2007/2008. They concluded that the two regions reacted differently during elections. It was clear that in the 2007/08 violence, Gusii proved to be peaceful, a scenario that saw many people from other parts of the country seek refuge there. Indeed, Kisii Town was initially a sleeping giant. It was woken up by the rise of population occasioned by the influx of people from various communities and with business interests who had been ejected from or were uncomfortable to stay in parts of the Rift Valley and Nyanza.

I left the meeting a more informed and determined man. Once home, I organized various peace meetings especially along the Bomet-Nyamira border. The meetings were attended by both Abagusii and Kipsigis who reside there. We discussed in detail why it was important to uphold peace and never let politics tear us apart.

I have to note that these meetings were successful because I received massive support from various people in the community. These people included Maati Ooga from Magombo-Isoge and elder Edward Bikundo from Kitutu Central. Others were Stanley Ondara, Joseph Mose, Nyaroo Osiemo and Sabastian Onyambu. They facilitated the penetration of Uwiano in this area by mobilizing residents to attend meetings and I will be forever grateful to them.

I have also been to Kisumu for peace meetings that left me more enlightened. I believe that peace is not costly but lack of it is very expensive. In the 2007/08 violence, Kenya lost many lives and the country suffered billions of shillings economic loss, all within days. In the process, children were orphaned and women widowed due to the violence. Several families were displaced and have never risen to recover the wealth they lost. I will never want my country to walk that path again. This is why I will always go out of my way to preach peace to all Kenyans.

# Nyamecheo Water Project & Water Matters

It has been argued at international platforms that the next world war will be over water. This argument sends cold shivers down my spine. Indeed, water is life. However, that this all important resource is becoming scarce over time is not news. This is a worrying scenario. I was born at a time when rivers, springs and streams in Gusii had huge volumes of water. During rainy seasons, some of the rivers and streams could overflow and claim lives.

However, due to an upsurge of population and other human activities such as the use of chemicals in farming, encroachment of water sources and planting of eucalyptus trees along rivers, the volumes of this resource has drastically reduced. Equally, the rain patterns have changed over time. Some springs in Gusii have disappeared. It is sad that some springs which had water throughout the year have since become seasonal. For example in 1968, Mzee Nyaroo drowned in a river near my home. That river is now a rivulet. It is now not strange to see the bed of a river like Gucha that was synonymous with flooding during the rainy seasons back in my days of youth.

When Kenya became independent, the architects of the nation envisioned a situation where every Kenyan would have access to clean and safe water for drinking. The deadline for realizing the goal keeps changing. At one time, the goal of access to clean water for all was meant to be realised by the year 2000. Two decades after that deadline, the goal remains a mirage. It is sad that, close to six decades after Kenya became a nation, many families do not have access to this essential commodity. Worse still, the original vision appears elusive. Indeed, many Kenyans especially in the northern parts of the country starve to death due to lack of water and food. Equally, crops wither and their animals die because they cannot find water. Water is life!

Sadly, time and again, Kenya experiences above normal rainfall. When this happens, the floodwaters claim lives and sweep property downstream. We watch as the water goes to waste, only to cry of drought weeks later when the rain is gone. This is strange to me. If we had our priorities right, Kenya, and particularly Gusii, would not lack water. In my thinking, every family needs to have access to clean piped water or at least be able to get the commodity within a radius of 1 km from their homes.

From the time I was the headmaster of Nyansiongo Primary School, I had interest in improved and reliable supply of water. This is why I took it upon myself to prepare the piping of water from Chief Onchera's plot for the commodity to reach Mecheo Primary School. The water came through gravity to be used by the school fraternity and the surrounding families. Members of Mecheo SDA Church also used it to make bricks with which we built a new house of worship for the Lord.

When the water was piped, many families found a reason to smile. Previously, they covered long distances in search of the resource from unprotected springs and streams. The piping was eventually extended from Manga scheme to benefit more families. The families of James Omariba and the late Onyambu were among the first ones to benefit.

Families enjoyed the benefits from this project but not for long. Some people who were guided by malice destroyed the pipes, cutting the flow of the water. Following this, some people took over the running of the project and they diverted the catchment to benefit different people. This move was scuttled later when it was discovered that the water was contaminated by waste from pit latrines. Due to the high levels of fecal content, public health officers condemned the water as unsuitable for human consumption. Unfortunately, some people use the water to this day despite the advice.

To revive access of piped water for the Mecheo community, pipes were laid from Gesima Scheme. This project was envisioned to bring water from the late Stanley Ondoro's farm. Along the line from the farms of the late Stanley Ondoro and Joseph Mose, the extension connected Mecheo Primary School to the water project. This also benefitted the families of Osiemo Nyaroo, James Omariba and Sebastian Onyambu. When I was transferred from Nyansiongo to Kisii Primary School, maintenance of the project became difficult. On top of that, outcasts vandalized the pipes and this made the project to collapse.

Since the project was close to my heart, I never got tired. I went ahead to look for ways of replacing and repairing the damaged pipes so that the water could flow again. In this endeavour, I mobilized members of the community from Mecheo and Gesima to revive the project. In our deliberations, we agreed to upscale the project so that it could benefit more people. This way, we thought that the number of those feeling that they were part of it would increase, which would also be a form of 'insurance' for the project from vandals.

For us to move forward, we formed an outfit that we named Nyamecheo Water Provider Association. This association was successfully registered by the Registrar of Societies and a certificate issued to us. I served as the Chairman, with James Ogata being the Secretary and Tabitha Omariba the Treasurer. Meshack Nyagwencha held the position of Assistant Secretary. Haron Mogi was one of the members.

Further, the Ministry of Water accepted to task the Lake Victoria South Water Services Board (LVSWSB) to make all possible arrangements to supply water to us from Nyaibaso spring. The board was also asked to rehabilitate Endemu Dam which sits on a 5.4 acre piece of land. Work on both projects (Nyaibaso spring and Endemu Dam) started simultaneously. This excited us but the works stalled midway to this day.

Although the board was mandated to undertake the project, I separately managed to access support from other quarters. For example, when I represented Kenya in the World Water Day celebrations in Dar es Salaam, Tanzania, I was given water pipes and a pump which I brought home for my community project. At the celebrations that were attended by delegates from member states of the Nile Basin, I closely mingled with the organizers and gave them the picture of the water situation back home. This impressed them and they included me in the list of Eminent Elders of the Nile Basin Initiative.

*****

While in Dar es Salaam, I gave suggestions on the use of water from various zones in Kenya. For instance, I suggested that water from River Nzoia and Yala should be utilized for irrigation. I also suggested that River Gucha, which navigates through the rich agrarian hills and valleys of Nyamira and Kisii then snakes down to Lake Victoria, should be properly used by people at the mother counties. I also noted that huge volumes of water in the Mara River ended in Tanzania while Lake Albert turned to Uganda.

I observed that the feeders of River Nile were turned to River Congo. Further, I underscored the point that overusing and diverting rivers that channelled their water to Lake Victoria reduced volumes at the water mass. This, I argued, had exposed rocks in the lake, making people to claim that those were islands like Migingo. In my thinking, when the levels of water in Lake Victoria went down, the volumes at the Nile equally reduced. In the long run, the Egyptians were affected as they could not get the quantity of water they needed.

The Egyptians had accused the ten countries of East Africa of reducing waters of River Nile. In protest, Egypt took the case to the International Court. The Egyptians based their case on the agreement signed between the British Empire and the Egyptian Government in 1929. The agreement was signed at a time when no country had attempted to extract water from the Mediterranean Sea through Egypt. Truly, the ten sister countries were using the water for their domestic use in the understanding that this was a God given resource.

Over time, the Egyptian government withdrew the case and tendered an apology. However, their decision was, to some extent, informed by the change of water volumes at the source. Those of us who participated and advanced the idea of utilizing water at the source were rewarded as Eminent Elders of East Africa. This recognition at the Milimani City Conference Centre in the heart of Dar es Salaam event, between 6th and 8th December 2009, is firmly ingrained in my memory.

The recognition aside, as indicated, I was also given several pipes and water pumps. On top of that, I was promised that people living within an area measuring 27 square kilometres in my immediate community would be assisted to get access to piped water at all times.

When I returned from Dar es Salaam, people back home were very happy for my active role at the international event. Due to this, they elected me as the chairman for dams rehabilitation in Borabu District. The twelve dams were constructed by the white settlers in colonial times and would address water challenges in the area if we rehabilitated them. Other officials in the committee included the Secretary Zephaniah Nyareru, Alice Monari, Johncyrus Ong'eta, Esther Nyagesira, Jackson Nyatwong'i, Thomas Nyangeri and Joachim Amenya. However, we have not made much progress because people have encroached on some of the dams and converted them into cultivable land. My dream for clean, safe and reliable water for the people of Mecheo is unchanged.

# Lighting Homes

In my days of youth, living in a house that had electricity spoke volumes about one's status. However important electricity is, very few people could afford it. Over time, some politicians tossed it as bait whenever they wanted to win an election. The Kenya Power and Lighting Company (KPLC) enjoyed, and still enjoys a monopoly of the distribution of the commodity to the extent that it appeared that Kenyans were at the mercy of the outfit. In the run-up to elections, the company would be used by politicians to show signs that an area would be connected to power by availing electricity poles and cables there. This made residents believe that they would soon be connected to the grid. In turn, they would vote for the candidate seen to be behind the plans to the last man. Invariably, after the election, the company would take its poles and leave the area in darkness.

Most parts of Kisii and Nyamira lacked electricity for many years. In fact, electricity was not a priority to many, due to the complexities that were involved in getting connected. I recall that the first electricity line in West Sotik was designed from Sotik to Chepilat and was to go along the border with Bomet, largely to benefit people on the Bomet side. The undertaking was spearheaded by an engineer who was a friend to Paul Soi. At the time, Soi worked as the District Education Officer in Kisii.

Soi and I worked closely and enjoyed a cordial relationship, although I was based in Siaya. Due to this friendship, it was not difficult for me to impart on him the need for schools in Borabu to be connected to electricity. When he appeared interested and willing to yield to the request, I listed the schools to be prioritized and they included Cheibing'ombe and Mecheo Secondary Schools.

At the time, a District Education Officer was a very powerful person. But for Soi, he was even more powerful because he hailed from the Kalenjin community and, 'one of their own', Daniel arap Moi was the Head of State. Soi promised to pursue the matter with the Kenya Power and Lighting Company and within a short period, the two schools got connected to electricity.

When I came home from Siaya, I found engineers at Mecheo Secondary School. They were preparing to mount a power transformer at the playground. I thought that the site was not ideal as it would lead to the underutilization of the field. Consequently, I advised the workers to put the transformer at an alternative spot within the school.

I had come for the weekend. I returned to Siaya, excited that it would not take long before my home got connected as well. However, when I came home the next time, I found that the transformer had been moved quite a distance away. It was now standing at the market, far off from the vicinity of the school. As a result, I could not get my home connected to electricity easily as I had imagined.

I thought that, although I had given the engineers a wise opinion to move the transformer a little from the playground, they may have been wiser to settle for the market. As a result, I could not interfere with the installation. Instead, I embarked on looking for the possibility of getting the main power line near my residence.

This undertaking was not likely to be possible without a sweat. However, I had separately started the water supply project for the neighbourhood. Since the project would need more power, I used it as an excuse to request the electricity distributor to install another transformer at Nyaibaso Market. The transformer would step-up electricity to pump water from a nearby spring. Due to the distance from my place of work in Siaya, I tasked some people in my area to attach the water project proposal to the request letter and deliver it to the officer in charge at the Kenya Power and Lighting Company offices.

Having understood and appreciated why our area needed to be connected to electricity, residents including Andrew Maati, Harun Obara, Duke Misati, Charles Ong'eni, Benson Mang'aa and Christopher Mokaya seized the matter and ran with it. After holding meetings in Keroka, they were able to liaise with the company for the work to start. However, as I came to learn, their efforts were thwarted, at some stage, when some individuals waylaid and attacked an engineer from the company while he surveyed our area. The engineer returned to his office in Kisumu with a negative report that threw the plans into jeopardy.

However, we did not lose hope. We resolved that it was prudent for us to stay focused and achieve our vision despite the bottlenecks laid on our way. With this spirit, we sent a delegation to Kisumu to meet the engineer and plead with him. We wanted to assure him that his security would be guaranteed. But, at Kisumu, we were informed that he was on leave at his Kendu Bay home. This compelled the delegation to hire a vehicle and trace his home.

The journey did not take long but when the delegation got to his home, he appeared not interested to get back to our place again. This was due to the way he had been manhandled during his earlier visit. However, after some deliberations, he yielded to the request of the group and came to the ground soon after to have us connected to electricity. Having drawn the electricity line map, the company delivered poles, cables and other installation items. Soon after, our area got lit!

Around the same time, the company's office in Kisumu also approved the installation of another transformer a stone throw away from my house. The company's officers had arrived at this decision after they realized that I had made immeasurable efforts to ensure the commodity got to the area right from Sotik, several kilometres away.

Once the transformers were installed and a number of homes including mine got connected, many people equally got interested. Presently, several homes in my neighbourhood are connected to the national electricity grid. However, there are some areas in the neighbourhood that have not been connected and I am certain that they too will, in due course.

My home is in a rural area and movement is minimal at night. Due to this, street lighting does not appear to be a priority. However, my feeling is that for security purposes, there should be high mast lights especially at shopping centers, market places and junctions. Equally, the solar lighting project by the County Government that has benefitted market centres should be cascaded to cover more areas across Nyamira. This way, the economy of the village will thrive as traders can run their businesses for longer hours.

I have to salute the government for taking electricity to the people in recent years. Indeed, during President Mwai Kibaki's tenure, the government did a lot to unlock the potential of the people by taking electricity to them. Right now, many businesses especially in the informal (*juakali*) sector are thriving in the countryside because of enhanced access to electricity.

Ambitious projects like the Last Mile Project have increased the level of Kenyans' access to electricity. The project has used the approach of installing transformers at public institutions like schools, from whence homes within a radius of 600 meters get connected at affordable rates. This has made electricity which was previously presumed to be a preserve of the elite to be a necessity for all.

However, I still think that the government can do more in ensuring that every home in the country is connected to electricity. This is more so due to the fact that, once installed and properly used, electricity is cheaper and cleaner than other forms of energy like kerosene and charcoal. The government should also invest more in tapping energy from other sources like solar and wind and reduce the charges passed on to the consumers of the commodity.

# Tarmac Road

To unlock the potential of any part of the country, a good road network is essential. However, over time, following independence, it appeared that development in Kenya was skewed to some regions. The prevailing situation made other parts of the country to lag behind economically. For instance, Borabu Settlement Scheme has been a sleeping economic giant. For a long time, we have had to contend with a poor road network, and thus failed to fully unlock the potential of the scheme. Indeed, save for the Chepilat-Keroka road that cuts through parts of the settlement scheme, there was no other tarmac road in the area until recently.

Being a border region, Borabu has had its fair share of challenges. Most roads in the area could not be passable during the rains. Cattle theft has been a major issue of concern in the area too. This evil persisted because the raiders could strike in the dead of the night and make away with animals through paths that were not motorable. The poor road network complicated recovery of the animals since the police could not respond promptly to pursue rustlers. For too long, we bemoaned that the security road in our area deserved to be all-weather and our tribulations and requests often hit the dead end.

My happiness is that the situation changed for the better. After President Uhuru Kenyatta retained his seat in the 2017 general elections, albeit amid controversies, I thought it would be a perfect time for his government to end the misery of the people of West Sotik by allocating funds for a murram road. I did not have direct access to the President, just like many Kenyans don't. However, I knew that he would jump on the idea once he got the word of it. I needed to link our request for help with some historical context.

*****

It is worth noting that historically, the Kikuyu and Kisii communities enjoyed a cordial relationship. In fact, during the struggle for independence, Jomo Kenyatta who later became the first President of the independent Kenya slid off the jaws of the British soldiers in Central region and sought refuge in Kisii. During this time, he was secretly hosted by the community's leaders like Chief Musa Nyandusi of Nyaribari.

Although Nyandusi was a sympathiser of the independence movement and hence Kenyatta, he was an official of the colonial administration. By virtue of this, he stood a chance of getting punished for harbouring Kenyatta from the pursuers. Due to fear that the intelligence would leak and plunge him into a hot soup, Nyandusi secretly organised for Kenyatta to be evacuated to a safer place within Kisii where the colonial administration would not imagine the freedom fighter to be hiding.

Due to this hide and seek game, Kenyatta settled in a number of places, including Mongorisi near my home. At that time, we could hear our parents talking in hushed tones that Kenyatta was around. We could overhear how, at night he would be hosted in a home that was never easily disclosed. When he was eventually discovered by the British soldiers and taken away, Kenyatta reportedly told his community (the Agikuyu) that Abagusii were good brothers who would be trusted in thick and thin moments. He further told them that remnants of the Agikuyu community's warriors would find it safe if they settled in Kisii.

In view of this, and in my own understanding, I felt that such a story would interest Kenyatta's son Uhuru who was now our president. I therefore approached Araka Matundura, the Chairman of Abagusii Cultural Elders' Council and requested him to hook me up with the President. Matundura is not new to me. I met him when he worked as a chief under the defunct Provincial Administration in Nyaribari Masaba. At the time, I was an education officer in Kisii and we needed each other in serving the people who fell within his area of jurisdiction. Additionally, as members of the Abagusii Elders' Council, we have shared severally on other issues meant to shape the destiny of our people.

It is important to note that after the 2017 elections, Kenyans were divided down the middle. The divisions emerged due to a discredited presidential poll outcome. Kenyatta had been controversially declared the winner, a matter that his closest contender Raila Odinga objected to. The electoral dispute ended up in court where the Supreme Court, under Justice David Maraga, ruled in favour of the petitioner, Raila Odinga, the NASA Presidential candidate. However, after nullifying the results and ordering a rerun, Odinga boycotted the exercise, claiming that the playfield was tilted in favour of Kenyatta. Odinga would shortly be 'sworn in' by his disgruntled supporters as the People's President, a matter that appeared to escalate the leadership crisis.

On the ground, our people retained the Kenyatta-Raila rift in their hearts. Some were diehard supporters of Kenyatta while others believed that the President had unfairly snatched Odinga's victory yet again. This scenario saw the economy head south. But within a short time, the two leaders closed the gap between them in what came to be called the Handshake. Progressively, the handshake bore the Building the Bridges Initiative (BBI) which seeks to find ways of avoiding a repeat of such acrimonious situations and build a one cohesive and indivisible nation, Kenya.

Prior to the handshake, thousands of people from the Kisii community held firm reservations against the President. This was rightly so because it was believed that Odinga enjoyed considerably more support in the region than did the president. But there was a bitter pill for our community to swallow; Kenyatta was the substantive president and this was validated once he got sworn in following the rerun. Therefore, they had no option other than accepting him.

*****

When I met Araka Matundura, I told him that it was prudent for the elders' council to initiate the healing process so that our people would accommodate the president. Frankly, Matundura had the way and the key, or so I believed. And I was right. We needed to invite the president to Gusii, where we would have him installed as our community elder. He would also hold a series of roadside meetings. This idea pleased Matundura. However, there was a problem; our community had elected governors (John Nyagarama-Nyamira and James Ongwae- Kisii) from Odinga's party, the Orange Democratic Movement (ODM). In the current Kenyan setting, governors are the Sheriffs at the counties. Matundura and I knew that it would be unreasonable to risk swimming against the local political wave on a matter of such magnitude.

Matundura told me that it would take ages for me to convince Ongwae to receive Kenyatta and be present in a function where the president would be installed as an elder of the community. His fears were anchored on the fact that Ongwae has had a long journey with Odinga, having served as the Orange Democratic Movement (ODM) Executive Officer. Matundura further indicated that although Nyagarama would be easier to convince, he would not spearhead the process of installing the president as an elder within the borders of Nyamira since he (Matundura) hails from Kisii. Indeed, he was right. Such an issue may look small but it bears huge ramifications politically. He was afraid that it could backfire on him as a man imposing leaders on the people of Nyamira.

To unlock this puzzle, I told Matundura that since I was his representative in Borabu, I would lead the installation ceremony if he granted permission. "That's very good. You have my blessings," he said. I was very happy but equally apprehensive. I had never had such an honour and I did not know how it would pan out. I had to ensure that I did the right thing.

The following day, I visited the Borabu Sub County Commissioner and shared with him the plans we had and he gave me a green light to continue. I also shared the same plans with the then Nyamira County Commissioner who told me, "if our boss and head of state will be installed as an elder of Omogusii, who am I to refuse? This is an act that will make our work easier as the President's eyes on the ground." He added that the matter will be captured in the itinerary of the president during his visit and the provincial security apparatus had taken note.

With the blessings of the president's field officers, I embarked on finding the traditional three-legged stool upon which he would sit. This would symbolize his acceptance as the elder of our community. I worked closely with other members of the Abagusii Cultural Elders Council, Borabu Branch, to get the stool and plan how the actual installation of President Kenyatta as an elder of Omogusii would be executed. We also agreed that it would take place at Kijauri grounds, not far from the Borabu Sub County offices.

On the material day, residents turned up in their numbers. Governors Nyagarama and his Kisii counterpart Ongwae were also in attendance.

I had a secret that I kept close to my chest. With the help of a few members of the community, we had prepared a memorandum addressed to the president. In it, we noted with humility that our area urgently needed to have a major road upgraded from earthen to tarmac standards. The road would start from Kijauri junction along the Kisii-Chepilat highway. It would then go through Nyansiongo, Manga, Raitigo, Chepng'ombe, and Mecheo and terminate Metamaywa.

When the opportunity provided itself, I got excited and equally anxious. The eyes of the President, his entourage and members of the public were all riveted on me. In my heart, I convinced myself that I was up to task and everything would go as planned. As I installed President Kenyatta as an elder of my community, cameramen clicked away while the onlookers clapped their hands. There were ululations and whistles too.

As this went on, I passed the memorandum to President Kenyatta, while whispering to him what it entailed in a summary. "*Mzee*, I assure you that the road will be allocated funds and works will start soon. You have done me proud and I promise to reciprocate," he said. By my side were church leaders such as Pastor Stanley Nyachieo and Pastor John Manani who presented the President to God through prayers.

Interior Cabinet Secretary, Dr. Fred Matiang'i, who coincidentally traces his roots to Borabu, was also installed as the community leader. Among other things, he was given a staff. This symbolically meant that Dr. Matiang'i is a notable figure, a messenger or servant that our community had sent to work with the President and bring us goodies in terms of development.

The presidency is a national asset. Therefore, the occupant of the position is closely guarded. His travel plans are jealously guarded by his handlers. This is to the extent that the plans can be changed at any given time without prior notice. For instance, on this day, the presidential helicopter was not far from the installation venue and I thought he was going to use it to fly to his next stop in Kisii. But after the symbolic ceremony, President Kenyatta announced that he was going to travel by road to meet the people. And indeed, he did so.

I noted earlier that the road I had in mind starts from Metamaywa. The starting point is barely two kilometres from Kijauri and therefore, the Presidential motorcade did not take long to get there. In his roadside address at the junction, President Kenyatta announced that the road project would start soon.

True to his word, it did not take long before a contractor moved to the site. This set residents wild with excitement. However, the works could not take off and move fast enough. Due to the snail-paced operations of the contractor who seemed to lack capacity, we got disgruntled and loudly worried how long it would take him to finish the project.

I went back to Matundura and gave him a picture of what was happening on the ground. Through Matundura, the Office of the President was brought up to speed as far as the status of the project was concerned. In a few days' time, the road was assigned to a different contractor who moved to the site quickly and started the works. I am grateful to Senator Okong'o o'Mogeni. He assisted the contractor to find a place where the construction workers would stay at Tindereti. I believe that the contractor will complete the project within the deadline given. Unfortunately for now, this is an ongoing project and I cannot celebrate its anticipated completion in the confines of this book.

**Biographer's Note:** *The road works of the said road were ongoing at the time of writing this book. However, the works appeared to move at a rather slow pace, largely due to the large amount of rainfall the area experienced late 2019 and early 2020. The roads are on pages 222 to 225.*

# Pilgrimage to Israel

Early in the morning of June 9th, 2013, I took a flight from Jomo Kenyatta International Airport (JKIA) destined for Cairo, Egypt. Aboard the Egyptian Airways plane with me was my wife Elizabeth and about sixty other members of the SDA church, drawn from various conferences, Nyamira included. This not being a chartered trip, there were tens of other travelers who were total strangers to me.

The take-off happened at 5 am. However, the journey had started weeks earlier, when my son Zablon informed me that he would cater for our expenses to visit the 'Holy Land'. I had felt a tiny tremor of excitement as I absorbed the news. The information equally whipped my wife into a fever of excitement. This was a great chance like no other and we instantly started preparations for the journey.

Since my wife's health was not in its perfect shape, I recommended to Zablon that it would be proper if a younger lady, preferably a close relative, accompanied us. Apart from playing the role of assistant to Elizabeth, the person would also help in showing her around. She would also answer any questions relevant to the trip that would linger in Elizabeth's mind.

As a family, we settled on my niece Esther Nyamweya. Apart from being a close relative, Esther was a teacher. She has since retired. We settled on her believing that she could give my wife sufficient company and assistance that would be beyond me while on the trip.

At the time, Esther served as the head teacher of Mecheo Primary School. When I delivered the news to her, she blushed with excitement and promised to marshal resources for the success of the trip. Esther would also take notes and record the places we visited while I took photos using a small point and shoot camera that we acquired for the purpose.

Really, I knew that it would not be a herculean task for Esther to raise the requisite funds for her air ticket and other logistics. Apart from being a teacher, she is blessed with children who are in meaningful employment. Equally, being an impromptu journey, my son chipped in to get Esther ready for the journey.

Having travelled to Arusha, Tanzania, before, I had a valid passport with me. This was not the case for Elizabeth. In fact, she had never been out of the country and we had never seen the need of her owning such a document. Now that the opportunity to travel had fronted itself, I swiftly moved to find the precious travel document for her right in time before the material day we set for travel.

With the assistance of a friend who was based in Kericho, I was able to process a birth certificate for my wife in record time. This enabled me to proceed to the nearest immigration office in Kisumu. (Presently, there is such office in Kisii and this has reduced the pain people from our region go through in possessing international travel documents.) Save for the long distance to Kisumu, I did not find much difficulty obtaining the document.

Soon, we were ready and embarked on the journey; and we all looked forward to the fun we would have.

The journey from JKIA was not without hitches. For example, it had been decided that since the few couples in the SDA entourage would be assigned common rooms while the rest would share, it was prudent for my wife and I to carry our luggage (mainly clothes) in one bag. This appeared wise until we got to the airport where the cabin crew said that the bag was too heavy and would only be transported as cargo. This would not only push the cost of travel but anxiety too on our side as first time and infrequent travelers. Imagine us arriving at the destination, which we knew little about, and starting to search for the cargo! To solve this, we packed part of our items in Esther's bag and we got cleared to travel with the bags as hand luggage.

The journey in the sky lasted about five hours but I do not remember sleeping during the entire flight. I kept imagining what the destination would look like. When the plane touched down in Cairo International Airport, we were warmly received by our Egyptian tour guides. In the team to receive us was Nadini of Temo Tours in whose buses we travelled in during most of the ground journey. We boarded the buses and proceeded for lunch at a hotel near a church. After lunch we proceeded to Giza District, west of the river Nile and visited the Giza pyramids. We marvelled at the pyramids of different sizes with a kind of order of seniority. The picturesque pyramids made of gigantic stones resting at a height of as much as 400 feet above the ground are still intact in my mind.

Other notable sites we visited during the pilgrimage included the hanging church which was built at a tower. This was initially built by Babylonians. We also saw the cave where Jesus was hidden by his parents as King Herod sought to kill all baby boys born at the time with the hope that one of these boys was Jesus. It was interesting to see and relate with the stories I had read in the Bible. A good example was the well where Jesus and his parents could draw water for their routine use.

My mouth waters when I recall the sumptuous meal we were served at a three storey revolving hotel on River Nile. We also visited the papyrus industry, and on this saw what is said to be the first handwritings of mankind.

On the next day, we began a journey of 480 Km towards the Suez Canal following the route used by the Israelites on the way from Egypt. We were lucky to pass through a well-constructed underground tunnel leading to the Sahara Desert, a place dominated by rocks.

Before the Red Sea, we had covered a road of 20 km through the rocks. It was 30 metres deep. We learnt that the place is called the Red Sea because the environment around it is red. The rocks lying below as well as the rocks surrounding it are all red and salty.

In the bus, excitement was evident as all of us hummed song after another. As a Christian, the experience just made me imagine what the journey to heaven would be upon Jesus' second coming. The tour guides did a perfect job, stopping the vehicle at every interval, either on their own volition (as per their schedule) or upon request to do so. This is how we managed to get close and see many other sites and take photographs.

My greatest luck was making it to Nazareth. This helped me to relate with the story of the birth of Jesus as expounded in the Holy Scriptures. This is where we saw huge paintings of the sheep and the shepherds and the workshop that is chronicled as the workplace of Joseph the father of Jesus.

I realized that although I subscribe to SDA teachings, the preservation of the heritage that is in Israel was largely done by the Roman Catholic. This is why there are many crosses in the place which is also inhabited by Muslims. I was also surprised to learn that, although Jesus was born in Bethlehem, his parents hid him from the enemies in Egypt, miles away.

When we travelled from Nazareth to Cana of Galilee, we visited the temple where Jesus changed water into wine during a wedding feast, the Mount of Blessings Church and the shore at the Sea of Galilee where Jesus met John and caught many fish. This is the same area where we witnessed the hexagon-shaped church where Peter saw Jesus walking on water and asked him to go to him.

Some of us in the entourage were not familiar with large bodies of water. The experience of crossing the sea aboard a boat was both exciting and frightening. Largely, there was a lot of excitement and jubilation as we crossed the sea and arrived on the other side of the shore. Once there, we were welcomed to lunch, mainly consisting of Galilean fish. After we had it to our satisfaction, we proceeded to River Jordan where Jesus conducted baptisms. Here, two of our members were baptized by Pastor Obongo. All the members in the entourage were very excited and hymns were sung in praise of our Lord Jesus Christ. It was the climax of the visit. We finished the day on a high note.

*Stephen Mabea*

*****

I deliberately chose not to mention every place we visited but I should note here that, apart from the religious perspective of the journey, I learnt a number of other things during the visit. For instance, I established that although Israel is largely a desert with almost 40% of its land covered with rocks, the country produces sufficient food to feed its population and export.

It is a testimony to the sophistication in the way they do agriculture. A good example is the farm we visited that had over one thousand heads of dairy cattle, taken care of by four men. In the milking area, the cows were arranged in sets, ready to be milked using automated machines. The milking was systematic and flowed seamlessly, with the milk getting tested and packaged, ready for the market in a matter of minutes. I was surprised that machines could run the show, right from feeding, washing the animals, milking and processing the milk, ready for dispatch to the market. This was unlike in Kenya where most farmers do all these things manually. Indeed, this could be one reason why our country does not have sufficient milk.

I also noticed that despite the fact that the country is largely dry, the Israelites do a lot of crop farming. In the country, agriculture is both an art and science. I could see acres and acres of crops like wheat and fruits of various varieties, neatly planted and tended. Due to mechanization, the farms are irrigated systematically and farmers make bumper harvests, season after season. For instance, I was surprised to see a farmer harvesting pawpaw fruit trees using a levered tractor with a lot of ease.

On June 15, we had our breakfast together and set off to St Catherine Monastery. While there, we saw the well of Moses and the burning bush. After going round the monastery, we started our journey back to Cairo through the South road along the Indian Ocean and passed though the capital town of Sinai via the Suez Canal back to Cairo and back to the Diplomat Hotel where we spent the night. The following morning, we went for shopping and later in the afternoon we boarded a plane back to JKIA.

I printed most of the photographs taken during the trip and I hold them dear. I also took some souvenirs, although I misplaced them later. I hope that one day; I will find them in the house.

**Biographer's Note:** *This section was compiled with input from Pastor Simon Obong'o and Esther Nyamweya who were part of the group that toured Israel with Mzee Mabea.*

# 7. CONCLUSION

## Where was my Family?

I thank God because He gave me a hardworking and focused wife. As a teacher and education administrator, I spent a substantial amount of time away from my family. Elizabeth played an active role during my absence from home. She was able to instil discipline in our children and mould them to be God-fearing and hardworking in education and other pursuits in life.

Today, teachers in Kenya are not highly paid. The situation was not any different when I got employed. However, I used my salary diligently to empower myself and those who directly and indirectly depended on me. Apart from investing on properties like land, a house and a car, I spent a reasonable share of my income to educate my children in boarding schools. During holidays, I stayed with them at home and gave them their time as a father. I listened and guided them accordingly. Because of the expansive nature of individual land at the settlement scheme, homes are situated far apart. So, my children spent most of their time in the compound and only got out when going to church or whenever we sent them.

My first born son Zablon set the pace for his siblings. He was a disciplined and diligent child who focused on his education. He was equally prayerful and respected his seniors and treated his siblings humanely. After high school, he secured a chance at the University of Nairobi where he studied Land Economics and Masters in Urban Management. This was a unique and highly competitive course at the time. He got employed by the Government almost immediately after he graduated. He had a progressive career, rising to the position of Commissioner of Lands, one of the senior most positions in the Ministry of Lands.

Zablon set the precedence for his siblings. Jane, Pamela, Roselyne, Barbra, Hyline, Caroline, Mong'are, Morebu and Aori walked in his footsteps. Most of them have first degrees while Aori is a PhD holder. They are all employed and have established their own families. Recently, Aori who is the last born child was appointed to the position of CEO of the Energy Regulators Association of East Africa (EREA).

In my community, family comes first. Wealth, power and anything else is secondary to the wellbeing of a family. We emphasize that whatever we do as parents should be in the best interest of one's spouse and children. Indeed, one's life is not measured by any yardstick other than the success, or otherwise, of the family he or she brought up. This strong attachment to family is not a preserve of the Kisii people but the majority of African communities.

When I look around, I pity the modern-day parent. Many children now exhibit unbecoming behaviour, sometimes under the watch of their parents. Some engage in drug and substance abuse and illicit sex. They do not hold their seniors in esteem as was the case in the old days. I think the worst blunder that we ever made as a nation is abolishing the cane as a form of disciplining children. Presently, some students treat their teachers as their equals and at times as their juniors. This has made teachers to stick to teaching and leave disciplinary matters to the parents. However, the truth of the matter is that discipline is integral in the success of the child. Ideally, therefore, teachers should be actively involved in ensuring that the young ones entrusted to them uphold high level discipline.

Some parents no longer mind the whereabouts and activities of their children. This cedes room for bad influence to thrive in the children. I believe it is the reason we hear of cases of arson, riots and other forms of unrest in schools.

This is what Mama Elizabeth Mabea said about her husband:

### Biographer's Note

*"My husband placed his pupils in the heart. Most of the time, he was away from home. Although Nyansiongo DEB Primary School is not very far from home, he usually came home for*

the weekend. At times, he went for two or three weeks before coming.

In his absence, I took full charge of the home. I was in charge of the discipline of our children. I fed them well and gave their father an update of their behaviour and progress when he came home.

I was in charge of farming activities too. We had pyrethrum and tea. I ensured the crops were well tendered, harvested and sold. At the end of the month, I received the earnings on behalf of the family.

At times, I made more money from the farm than my husband did from his job. One time, I earned a total of Sh80,000 from various farming activities. I gave the whole amount to my son Zablon and told him to keep it safe and make use of it to educate his siblings in case we left the world before they completed their education.

## Our School System

I have noted that in recent years, very few schools put emphasis on education. This is so because the government has made it compulsory for every student to be promoted to the next class irrespective of performance. When students realize that they do not need to beat some mark to be promoted, they do not see any reason of working hard in their studies. The situation is aggravated by the 100% transition rate from primary to secondary schools. Essentially what it means, the Kenya Certificate of Primary Education (KCPE) does not filter those who join secondary schools and those who should pursue other alternatives.

Discipline is basically self-control. Children should know that they have been taken to school to study and prepare for their own future. Therefore, they should shun laxity and make maximum use of their time and the learning resources availed to them. Naturally, though, students tend to work better when they are pushed to do so. This is why, as I stated earlier, abolishing the cane was a major blunder that elevated children to small gods. We have aped countries of the West but I am a firm believer that the Bible is right on this score when it says that, *"Don't hesitate to discipline children. A good spanking won't kill them,"- Proverbs 23:13, Good News Translation*. Equally, wise men say that if you spare the rod, you will spoil the child.

The foregoing notwithstanding, it is a fact that some teachers misused the cane, causing grievous harm to their students. This fuelled the debate that resulted in the withdrawal of the cane from schools. My view is that this was an irrational decision that should be revisited. The cane, if effectively used, is the most effective and easiest form of disciplining young people.

There seems to be a lot of changes in the sector of education. The country is moving away from the 8-4-4 system of education that has been in existence since 1985. The curriculum is being replaced by the 2-6-3-3-3, commonly referred to as the Competence Based Curriculum (CBC). This is not a bad idea. However, if the country does not approach the issue wisely, it may come to haunt us. There should be watertight modalities that would ensure a peaceful transition between the two curriculums.

About 200,000 youths graduate from our universities annually. However, and this is sad, the country is not able to produce job opportunities for these people. It is rather worrying that Kenya is increasingly harbouring thousands upon thousands of educated yet jobless people. It is my hope that the government will continue creating an enabling environment for the blue collar economy to thrive.

Kenya is a one indivisible nation comprised of 47 county governments. However, this is only true on paper; Kenyans often get divided along ethnic lines each time we go for a general election. Sadly again, although our elections are supposed to come after every five years, Kenya is in an electioneering mood all the time. This should not be the case. I think that were it not for divisive and retrogressive politics, Kenya would be one of the most cohesive and economically advanced nations in the world. I suggest that Kenyans root for practices like intermarriages, studying together and pursuing the greater dream of building a prosperous country. This way, we will be able to seal the gaps brought forth by tribalism.

When the country got independent, materialism was at the back burner of most Kenyans. Amassing wealth at the expense of others was perceived to be a bad habit. However, a few individuals in key positions quickly plundered public resources to enrich themselves. This set a bad precedent for other Kenyans. Indeed, it appears that corruption is getting increasingly entrenched amongst Kenyans where some believe that it is the only way of making it in life. This sad trend should be discouraged at all costs so that we build a nation for us all.

I believe that the school system can be used effectively to lay strong foundations of the Kenyan nation, devoid of corruption.

# If I Were to Reverse the Clock!

Just recently, my smart phone malfunctioned. For several days, I could not access WhatsApp which is a very good application that enables me to talk to my relatives across the world. Mobile telephones came the other day and I will be playing hide and seek with the truth if I say that I am well-versed with the gadgets. This is why I passed it to my son Mong'are to establish where the problem was. It did not take him a minute to tell me that the application had expired and needed to be reinstalled. He added that the phone was slow because it had been attacked by a virus. To fix the problem, he restored the phone to factory settings first, then remarked, "this phone will now work as if it is new." And it did!

As I reflected on this, I put my life in perspective and asked myself, "what if I became a child again? What would I do differently?" Then I jogged my mind down the memory lane, evaluating every stage of my life. At the end of it, I said that if I become a child today and God gives me a hundred or so years to live, I will live exactly the way I have lived.

This is to say, I do not hold any regrets in my life. I believe that I have lived my life the way I would have wished to live it. If there were mistakes that I ever committed to myself or to anyone, then they are too negligible to get me worried. I am not a perfect human being, but I have tried to live well. I believe that I have been a blessing to many people. I also believe that the many interactions I have had, have been of great blessing to me as well. This gives me the happiness that is fundamental at my age. I would be a very worried person if I ever knowingly wrongly punished or condemned anyone and destroyed his or her life.

Serving as a teacher and school administrator and eventually holding a substantive office at the district level is a major accomplishment for me. This is especially so when I consider where I started and the opportunities I had at the time. The career path I took enabled me to know very many people. I made many friends in the process. Some of my friends were my pupils; others were my co-workers and the many that I assisted to find a source of income. I therefore thank God for choosing this career path for me and enabling me to walk through it.

It is possible that, along the way, I did step on some people's feet unknowingly. If ever this happened, then such people either forgave me in silence or kept a grudge against me in secret. I hope that they all forgave me or will do so upon learning that I never intentended to wrong them.

Just when I had started my career as a teacher, I was tempted to leave my country and try life abroad. Quite frankly, I did not have a clear roadmap with me on what I intended to do once I got out there. This was a risky and illegal undertaking. I do not regret that it aborted, not once but twice. Indeed, some people who got a chance to pursue studies abroad returned home and led successful lives. For instance, my cousin Momanyi studied in Russia and upon return, joined the military as a medic. He eventually ventured into private practice and ran hospitals that did very well. Still, there are others who travelled abroad and missed opportunities. They returned home empty handed. Such people led miserable lives afterwards, perhaps full of regret. I do not know what would have happened to me if I too managed to get out of Kenya at that time. I thank God that I never did, for I have led a life that, though not very modest, has been very fulfilling.

I believe that when God gives you an opportunity to life, you have to live it to the fullest. There is no better way of living than taking care of your life and your family, and serving God and humanity. These are the beacons that I have used thus far. I retired from my professional work but I still have some energy that keeps me going, always hoping to touch others' lives. I will continue doing this as long as I am healthy and able.

My life hasn't been without challenges. I have been confronted with many of them over time. For instance, when I did well in my examinations at Motagara Intermediate

School and secured an admission at the African Government School, Kisii (now Kisii School), I thought that I had an opportunity to work hard and end up in university someday. However, when I got to the school, I was withdrawn (unfairly, I believe) and recommended for a certificate course in teaching at Kabianga Teacher Training College. Despite the drawback, I accepted the situation as it had come and went on to become a very good teacher, in my estimation.

I believe that in one's life, there comes a time when you take it as it comes. In retrospect, if I had rejected the offer, perhaps I would have taken a path that would have had debilitating effects on my life later. But again, it is hard to know what would have become of the 'path not taken'. Nevertheless, I studied as a private candidate and got a Form Four certificate. I went on and obtained the London General Certificate of Education (advanced level) and the Cambridge Advanced Certificate. I also received a letter of offer to pursue a degree at the Adult Kikuyuni Campus of the University of Nairobi but shelved the chance due to overwhelming commitments at work.

In the course of my professional work, I encountered some problems and frustrations that seemed to have been orchestrated by people whose motives appeared ulterior. For instance, the manner in which I was transferred from Kisii District to Siaya spoke volumes about men who seemed hell-bent on getting me off my career trajectory. I would have resisted and rightly so as it was well within my rights to protest. However, I realized that this would have given victory to the suspected detractors. As such, I refused to sit like a cry-baby and beg them for a change of heart. I just did not want to bend my principles. In the long run, a transfer that appeared meant to frustrate me made me stronger, smarter and wiser. It also expanded my networks and enriched my overall professional and life experiences. So, I have come to believe that problems are not there to break us. They only enhance our abilities and make us stronger. In fact, life on earth would not have meaning if it did not have challenges. In my view, these challenges make life worth living.

I believe that where I met obstacles, I tackled them the best way I could at that time. There were problems that needed one to go round, over or under them. Others needed one to 'plough' through them. However, there were others that were beyond my capacity to solve and I could do nothing about it. In this life, one can only change what is possible. If one forces things to happen, he could end up being the causality or, at the very least, frustrated.

The education sector today is a mess and a shadow of what it used to be. I look back and wonder who is behind this ever-increasing mess. Truth be told, the sector is in turmoil, what with compromised academic standards, demoralized and overworked teachers, and an overburdened and lazy student population. Today, the syllabus changes now and again. As a result, it confuses the learner and heightens the burden on the parent who must keep buying new books as recommended time after time. In my hay days, it took a fair number of years before a syllabus changed. This provided a stable teaching environment and allowed education to penetrate into the heads of the learners easily and more deeply than it happens today. Today, the syllabus is forever tentative and this lack of consistency in a digital world over time is unhealthy for the sector and nation at large.

As I hit the homestretch in telling my story, the world came to standstill, quite literally due to the Corona virus pandemic. The disease which was first reported in Wuhan (China) in 2019, fast spread to the rest of the world. In Kenya, the first case was reported in March 2020, forcing the government to take drastic measures to contain the virus. The measures included closing down all learning institutions from kindergarten up to universities.

This started less like a joke. We thought that the paralysis of our normal lives would only last a couple of weeks. However, as days passed, the cases of the disease continued to spike. This forced the government to count the 2020 education calendar year wasted. It means all students will repeat their classes in 2021. This has never happened before.

My happiness is, around mid-August, Kenya started to report fewer cases of Corona virus infections and deaths. I hope this trend will continue. However, the disease pattern is not yet clear. Some countries reported a decline of new cases for a couple of months before the cases rose again. I think the way out of the mess the world has found itself in will be the discovery of a vaccine. For now, I have to end my story, for I do not know how the education sector will cope in the future. I just hope that the government will put its act together and ensure that our education does not go to the dogs due to the confusion occasioned by the disease, as well as other new life challenges.

I must conclude my story by thanking the Almigthy God. Indeed, I have tasted His goodness (Psalms 34:8) for He has been my refuge. He is the true King of my life and that of my family. My journey from the very humble beginnings with the many challenges and certain occurrences can only be surmised as "divine appointments" meant to shape my life and all those who look upon me as their mentor.

## THE END!

www.ingramcontent.com/pod-product-compliance
Lightning Source LLC
Chambersburg PA
CBHW071403300426
44114CB00016B/2170